M000024945

LOVE IN THE EYE OF THE STORM

HURRICANE IRMA, SAINT MARTIN & TOGETHERNESS

BILLY NAHN ·

*For my wife, Shanie, whose strength
and courage know no bounds.*

Thank you to Marsha, Pete, and Janis, as well as dear family and friends who proofed and contributed their ideas and encouragements.

A special thank you to Arnaud Pages for the cover design, evocative cover photo and enthusiasm for this project.

PREFACE

Observing Shanie sitting on the floor, I flashback to when I found her sitting against a bathroom wall several days after her cancer surgery. She was alone. In the dark. Sobbing. The trauma of her bilateral mastectomy catching up to her. The physical and emotional pain and the confrontation with mortality all ripping away her core. The only way Shanie could battle against all of this was to wail away in the blackness of the room. I lightly rapped on our bathroom door, entered and sat beside her for the next hour or so, holding her, saying nothing. Her sobs finally giving way to slow and steady breathing.

This is how she looks now as the runaway locomotive train that is Irma continues thrashing everything outside. There is no letup as trees snap in half, unknown flying objects slam heavy against our exterior concrete walls, and the relentless winds hauntingly scream as they violently try to penetrate the steel hurricane shutters.

But, we are silent as the world comes noisily apart around us. Shanie does not cry or scream out. She has faced mortality before and was victorious. She is not afraid.

I'm terrified.

STAIRWAY TO HEAVEN

I wake sometime before midnight to an eerily quiet apartment, except for the faint sounds of someone moving about on the patio. I look over to Shanie who is fast asleep on the other twin mattress.

To not disturb her, I quietly get out of bed and slowly open the patio's sliding glass door. Unbeknownst to Alain, who is shirtless, and strumming an acoustic guitar strapped across his chest, I step outside to enjoy what he is playing as he peers out from his elevated vantage point of Villa Haiku. I think about the movie Titanic and the legend of the band still playing as the ship is sinking. He is playing the guitar and facing in the exact direction Irma will hit the island of Saint Martin.

It's easy to admire his moxie against the unknown onslaught barreling toward us. I know from his view, he can see how the landscape drops steeply from his driveway and eventually leads all the way to the ocean. It's a beautiful, yet surreal moment. Alain turns around and notices me on the patio ledge and makes his way back to sit next to me. He switches to another song, Led Zeppelin's, "Stairway to Heaven." Knowingly or not, he has just notched this surreal moment up another degree, but then he abruptly stops.

"No. No, don't... keep playing," I tell him, "you're really good." He restarts and is picking through the famous opening bars as I relay this is the first song my son, Skylar, ever learned on the guitar.

"Really, does he still play?" Alain asks as he progresses to the main riff of the song. I give him a brief review of Skylar's musical talent and desire to make a career as a musician. Alain continues to strum as the conversation slows until we just quietly sit for a several moments, fully aware that Irma is stampeding towards us. As if on cue, the winds subtly begin to announce her arrival on the island of Saint Martin.

Alain and I continue to sit on the edge of the patio listening to the ever-increasing sound of the wind.

"Can you hear it?" He asks me.

I listen intently and know exactly what Alain is referencing. It is a menacing roar growing, emanating from somewhere out in the darkness of the Caribbean Sea.

It is Irma.

A CELEBRATION OF BEING
FREE OF CANCER

-one week earlier-

My wife Shanie was diagnosed with breast cancer two months after our wedding. We had just moved to Scottsdale, Arizona from Madison, Wisconsin, for my new job as an Executive Producer at GoDaddy. With our new health insurance cards in hand, Shanie made an appointment for a check-up. This is when her cancer, DCIS, Ductal Carcinoma in Situ, was discovered in her right breast.

After family meetings, several discussions with the Arizona Breast Consultants and intensive research by both Shanie and her father, Rod, it was decided the best course of action would be a radical, bilateral mastectomy. Rod's two sisters had lost their battle with breast cancer and with that family history, it made sense to take an aggressive approach. She would have both breasts removed.

Those dark days of diagnosis, surgery and reconstruction combined with the shattering emotional and physical trauma of amputating parts of her body tested the strength of our new marriage. But Shanie has a deep well of courage and I have a deep well of optimism. So even through sobbing tears and fears of mortality, we stood by each other. There to lift one's spirit, there to hold a hand, there to just be there - quietly by each other's side. Oftentimes, not saying anything, just being present and reassuring. This early test in our marriage laid a diamond-hard foundation for our partnership.

We had skipped on our honeymoon to move to the southwest, so we put our official celebration on the back burner. Our thought was to wait for more free time, more resources and an opportunity we just couldn't pass up.

That opportunity arrived six years later. We would enjoy our postponed honeymoon and six years of being cancer-free with a month-long vacation on the Caribbean Island of Saint Martin.

A close friend of Shanie's had been shopping for real estate on the island, and invited her on a couple separate house hunting trips earlier that year. After those trips, Shanie had fallen "head over heels" in love with Saint Martin. It was her suggestion to go to the island for our honeymoon. She found a fantastic deal on a beautiful condo in the Anse Des Sables residential complex on the French west side of the island. This apartment building was perfectly located for two honeymooners. It was nestled on the water's edge of the Caribbean Sea and walking distance to both the town center of Marigot, and the quaint Marina Royale District.

Not in my wildest imagination, at 53 years of age, could I believe my wife and I would spend an entire month snorkeling blue waters and dining on wonderful French and Island cuisine. This would be the trip of a lifetime.

September for much of the Caribbean is considered the "Low Season or Off Season." For us, it meant fewer tourists, better rates on accommodations and a more casual feel on the island. Perhaps, a more realistic way to experience what the locals call, "island life." But there is another more unflattering moniker for this time of year on the island, "Hurricane Season." And for 2017, it would prove to be globally one of the most devastating.

It's 3:00 a.m. on the morning of our departure for Saint

Martin out of Sky Harbor in Phoenix, Arizona. I awaken before the iPhone alarm and decide the first order of the day is to consider a more appropriate travel outfit. Instead of being fashionable with French cut jean shorts and short sleeve shirt. I figured I better go more "Indiana Jones," ala cargo shorts with many pockets that have Velcro closures. I have a favorite pair that fits the bill, complete with a plethora of pockets to safely secure my passport, cash, Ridge wallet and iPhone.

I tightly roll up the jean shorts and stow them in my suitcase and then head directly to the kitchen and our beloved Bunn Flash Brew Coffee Maker; a genius machine that stores hot water at the ready. When I pour a carafe of new water into the machine, I instantly get scalding hot water flushing through my ground coffee beans. In our house, coffee is king and the sooner Shanie and I can have our first cups, the better. My wife's brew consists of a spoon full of Stevia, and topped off with chocolate-flavored soy milk. My cup is simpler, coffee and skim milk. I take a few sips and quickly feel my stomach turn in a way no one wants to experience when you are about to board a plane for a nine-hour flight. In disbelief, I hurry to the hallway bathroom.

The night before, we had a bon voyage party with Shanie's parents, Rod and Patti. We cooked pizzas, drank wine and excitedly talked about all the adventures awaiting my wife and I on the island of Saint Martin. The pizzas tasted fine and were the perfect meal to share laughs and a few healthy glasses of Malbec. Patti and Rod didn't stay too long. We retired early in the evening, knowing we had a 4:00 a.m. alarm.

I return from the bathroom to the kitchen and without any warning proceed to cough uncontrollably. Why I'm experiencing this horrible, unpleasant cough on this, of all mornings, is beyond me. Shanie calls out from the bedroom to check if I'm okay and I meekly reply, "Just something goofy with my stomach this morning." I head into the kitchen, hoping a bit more coffee will help. After a few more sips, I need to race down the hallway to the bathroom. This process occurs several times over the next forty-five minutes as Shanie keeps a watchful eye on me while finalizing her packing.

"Everything is fine." I try and reassure her between my frequent pilgrimages to the bathroom.

"It's just a little weak stomach or something. Nothing to worry about."

I've been fortunate to travel a good part of the world as an Executive Producer for GoDaddy. I would oversee the filming of TV commercials in Sri Lanka, Rio, Mumbai, South Africa, Mexico and the UK; and one of my biggest fears in all of those long flights and exotic locales is a foodborne problem. And today, it feels like it's what I'm dealing with. We are three hours before takeoff and know full well what lies ahead with long airport lines, cross country flights and public bathrooms. Concern is a gigantic understatement.

Our pre-arranged Uber driver arrives promptly at 5:30 a.m. and we load up our two suitcases, my trusted and traveled backpack, Shanie's purse and a pink and yellow colored carry-on. I lock the door to our home and once again feel my stomach turn. I sincerely hope I don't throw up in our Uber driver's new Hyundai Sonata.

The road out of Fountain Hills is slow and curvy which for some reason is comforting. Shanie, sitting in the back, goes into full conversation mode with our driver and uncovers he is a military veteran, a marine, who has served three tours in Afghanistan. Last year, he provided over 2,000 Uber rides and absolutely loves being an Uber driver. As my wife begins to relay our plans for the month on Saint Martin to him, I quietly hold everything together and am thankful the AC is on. I re-position the vent to blow more directly into my face.

We pull into the arrivals lane at Sky Harbor and effortlessly go through the Airport check in. With all my international travels for GoDaddy, I have Global Entry, which also means each airline ticket is also TSA Pre-Check. We glide through security.

Our gate, 23D, is located at the far end of the terminal. We pass by a Peet's Coffee Shop and Shanie mentions she would like a soy milk latte and a bottle of water. Always the conversationalist, my wife and the lady at the counter talk about Shanie's chunky emerald ring while waiting for her latte. Unfortunately, I have to make another stop to the bathroom.

It seems my digestive tract is not ready to embrace the idea of a nine-hour flight to St Martin. After several failed attempts to leave the bathroom stall. I breathe deeply and ponder leaving Shanie at the airport and try catching another flight the following day. But, I push the thought away and know that I have to figure something out. The idea bulb goes off. I will line my boxers with toilet paper. I can think of no other viable option. So I unfurl about four feet of TP, carefully folding it over and over, and in utter disbelief place that neat pile of TP between my boxers and my derriere. I take a deep breath and exit the bathroom stall. After some serious hand washing, I humbly walk out to the throngs of passengers in Terminal 4. In my mind, I believe everyone is looking at me, fully cognizant of my "MacGyvered Depends."

I still don't feel any better, so Shanie hands me a couple Imodium pills. Either psychosomatically or physically, they have an immediate and positive effect. But, not taking any chances, I keep my TP snug in its current location.

The gate agent makes an announcement that our plane is ready to board. As we stand in line, I close my eyes and make a wish that I don't embarrass myself, my wife or anybody else as we fly across the country on an American Airlines Boeing 737.

Much to my surprise and more so, my relief, I actually sleep quite a bit on the flight to Miami. After a brief delay, we are on our way to Princess Juliana International Airport on the Island of Saint Martin. It's a little more than a 2-hour flight from Miami. And by the graces of good fortune, but more likely the Imodium, my digestive system is back to normal.

Saint Martin is a single island controlled by two countries. The French and the Dutch. Which also means the island has two different spellings, for albeit the same name. The French call it Saint Martin, the Dutch, Sint Maarten. The island is basically split North and South. North is governed by France and the south is an independent nation of the Netherlands. The traditional story is that a Frenchman and a Dutchman had a walking duel. They stood back-to-back in the middle of the island as the Frenchman walked north, the Dutchman walked south. As the tale goes, the Frenchman walked farther amassing more territory because the Dutchman kept stopping for drinks along the way. I'm sure there are other variations about this tale, but it's hard to blame the Dutchman for stopping and socializing along the way. It is a Caribbean island after all and Saint Martin is internationally known as the "Friendly Island."

Princess Julianne International Airport is on the southwestern tip of the island and operated by the Dutch government. It all seems overly confusing to me as we stand in the immigration line as to who owns what and who is responsible for their part of the island. Nevertheless, we breeze through Immigration and receive our passport stamps. We make our way to the baggage carousel for our luggage. I notice a fellow traveler over by a SIM card kiosk. She is unsuccessfully trying to put dollars into the automated machine. The kiosk seems to be broken. Before we left for the island, my son, Finley, a junior in college, advised I get a local SIM card for my iPhone. But, I'm tired from my mornings bathroom adventure and the day of travel so, I pass on getting a local SIM card. A decision I would later deeply, deeply regret.

After picking up our two suitcases, we exit the terminal and head to the taxi queue. The airport feels more like a regional airport than an international one. The taxi line is just a few steps outside the arrivals' doors. Shanie heads to a taxi van as the driver exits. He makes no eye contact, but loads our suitcases.

"Anse Des Sables," she tells him. He just nods in approval.

It's now 10:00 p.m. and this is my first look at Saint Martin. The air is warm and filled with the sweet smell of the tropics. It's all new to me so I am wide-eyed, taking in all the sights like a four-year old looking at Christmas presents under the tree. We travel along Airport Road and across the Simpson Bay Causeway Bridge. The bridge is beautifully lit with lamp posts across its span and creates a wonderful strobe light effect as we drive under each lamp on the empty roadway. Shanie and I gaze out the van's windows and enjoy the sparse harbor lights and the illuminated masts from a fleet of sailboats moored in the bay.

It's only a 15-minute drive from the airport to our complex, located on the edge of Marigot and next to the Marina Royale District. Estelle, the condo owner, meets us at the Anse Des Sables security gate. She is a pretty and petite French lady. Her Dorothy Hamill haircut bobs in the glow from the swimming pool lights as she escorts us into the complex. We climb up three levels of a wide brick staircase to our apartment where we'll spend the entire month of September. It is number 90 and located on the right side of a long wing of the complex. She unlocks the door and the light from the condo spills into the hallway. She leads us into a clean, modern-looking studio. The narrow entry way reveals to be actually part of the galley kitchen. The door to the right of the kitchen sink opens to a spacious bathroom with a glass-lined shower, sink and toilet.

The entryway/kitchen galley is about ten-feet in length that then opens up into the large bedroom and living area. There is a king bed, a gray couch, modern white table with storage drawers, and another white, short storage shelf with a TV perched atop. Double patio doors next to the couch open up to a small porch complete with bistro table and two white folding chairs. The view from the deck includes the swimming pool and directly across the street, a lighted soccer field. To the left of the soccer field begins the Marina Royale district and tall masts rock to the unseen motion of the harbor waters. This is paradise.

Estelle's husband gets up from the couch to greet us. Instantly, I like him with his bright eyes and big smile. For the next 20 minutes, they show us their beautiful studio. She instructs us on the WIFI password, the TV remote and what channels are English, including CNN. If we have any questions, Estelle requests we call her on WhatsApp.

Shanie had prepared a few bank envelops priort to the trip and I hand one to Estelle which has $1,000 written across the seal with a black Sharpie. This is our payment for the condo. Because of our expected late arrival, and that many of the local shops close around 9:00 p.m., Shanie inquired if Estelle would purchase a couple bottles of Bordeaux, cheese and baguettes for our first night on the island.

Before Estelle and her husband leave, they hand us the wine opener. I uncork the Bordeaux, let it breathe for moment, then pour a deep amount into crystal glasses.

For Shanie and I, our honeymoon is just starting.

Unfortunately, also starting across the Atlantic near the Cabo Verde Islands of Africa is Hurricane Irma. Or, more aptly named in this part of the world, Cyclone Irma.

HONEYMOON ISLAND

For me, it's always fun and exciting to arrive at a new destination during the night and awaken to all the surroundings revealed to you by the color of daylight. This anticipation to see this Caribbean Island with crystal blue seas, lush green rainforests, white sandy beaches, and new adventures is all I need to guarantee I'll be up by first light.

As daylight creeps through the curtains, I hop out of bed and quietly explore the kitchen to prep coffee for brewing. The ground coffee, filters and automatic drip are easy to locate and without much fuss, the slumber-killing aroma drifts quickly throughout the small condo and envelops Shanie. This magical, aromatic effect causes my wife to reluctantly stir from her childlike sleeping pose.

"Is it morning already?" She softly murmurs.

"Just about, and we have an island and 30 days to get rolling," I reply with a large mug of coffee in hopes of expediting the days' escapades.

"Open the curtains and patio doors, I want to see and feel the air," she beckons.

As I open the patio doors, we are presented with the glory of a Caribbean sunrise. The clean, ocean air quickly enters our condo as well as the early light. It's a warm hue cascading over my beautiful wife as she stretches across the king size bed. She is radiant.

"I told you this place is magical."

"Wow. Wow. Wow." Is all I can reply.

Our third-floor patio is tucked into the corner of the L-shaped design of the Anse Des Sables complex. From our patio's deck, I can see all the patios that run parallel along the road as well as the patios of the shorter wing. There are hanging towels, ice chests and other tell-tale signs that many of the units are occupied. The morning light also reveals more bobbing sailboat masts in the harbor than I could see last night. Their charming sight is accompanied by the pleasant and addicting clang of their stays and lines.

After we finish our coffee, we do a quick unpack of our suitcases. The condo has two floor-to ceiling-white closets. Shanie opens the door to one and sees that it is for storage. Inside are two beach chairs, a small beach umbrella and vacuum cleaner. The other is empty and has three shelves, plus a short hanging rod for clothes. Shanie capitalizes on this one. She quickly places her shorts, socks and swimwear on the shelves and then hangs her many sun dresses. Since the closet isn't large enough to stow all her belongings, she opts to leave an open suitcase next to the storage unit with the TV. I travel a little lighter and it doesn't take long to organize my stuff. I think it's always wise to hide some of our money, so I stuff an envelope in a water proof bag that I then place inside my snorkel gear swim bag. I hide this in cubby hole underneath the TV.

The next order of the morning is to walk into the Marigot Towne Center for a guided tour from Shanie and a stop at the "Super U" grocery store for supplies. As we move about the condo unpacking and organizing, I feel the increasing strength of the Caribbean sun.

"Do you know where we packed the sunblock?" I ask Shanie as she turns around from hanging a sun dress.

"It's in the bathroom on the shelf," she responds.

"Cools," I reply, heading into the bathroom. "Found it," I shout, returning to the living room.

"Let's bring some extra bags to carry the groceries," my wife suggests, laying a few out atop the bed.

"I've got my backpack as well."

She drapes a bag over her shoulder and places another one inside it as I put on my backpack and favorite green ball cap.

"All set?"

"Yep," Shanie replies with a big smile on her face. I can already see that she is in her element on the island and eager to share with me some of her favorite spots in Marigot.

We exit the condo, lock it up and head down the wide brick steps to the first floor. Since we are located on the street side of the complex, I make a quick detour to an exit on the Caribbean Sea side of the building. I open the door and haphazardly almost step into a pool of water. The entrance to the condo is guarded by a three-foot by three-foot inlaid foot wash. It's there to encourage people to rinse their feet prior to entering the building. In my haste to see the ocean, I almost plant both feet into the four-inch deep sandy water. After a quick adjustment, I stand on the edge of the foot wash and get my initial view of the Caribbean Sea that envelops Saint Martin. It is stunning. There is a short beach, about 15 yards between the sea and the ground floor units. Nobody is on the beach and, anchored several hundred yards out on the gentle blue waters, float several large catamarans and sailboats.

"This place is awesome."

Shanie smiles and then grabs my hand to lead me towards the main entrance of the condo.

"I need more coffee, so let's head into town. We'll come back and swim this afternoon."

"Alright, alright," I happily reply, closing the door.

We stroll along the sidewalk of Rue De Sandy Ground that leads into Marigot. Adjacent to the Anse Des Sables complex is the water front "Le Beach Hotel." The hotel is large with beautiful wrought iron, New Orleans style, gated patios, and a newer red tin roof complete with a large glass atrium. The double front doors to the lobby have been propped open, and as we stroll by the hotel, we look directly through the lobby to the Caribbean Sea and more sailboats anchored just off the shoreline.

Shanie and I walk hand-in-hand as we move off the sidewalk and across the hotel's parking lot to another sidewalk closer to the road. The traffic is light, consisting of a few high-revving mopeds and a couple of small sedans.

We cross the two-lane street to another sidewalk that allows us to stroll alongside the marina.

"That's where the sailing school is located," Shanie points to a closed-up shop that sits at the end of the block. The painted sign reads: "Maritime Sailing School of the West Indies." The front of the building faces the lagoon and has two long piers with several sailboats and a few smaller dinghies roped to cleats all along the two piers.

Before we departed for Saint Martin, we discussed registering for either a "Day Skipper" sailing course or a "Dingy Piloting" course from the academy. The courses are usually a week long and with our extended stay on the island, might be the perfect time to hone-up my nautical skills. We own a 27-foot pilot house sailboat docked in Dana Point, California and have plans of trading that boat for a larger one to sail around the Caribbean islands.

Shanie and I continue heading down Rue de Sandy Ground as it seamlessly becomes Rue de la Liberte. This route will take us into the heart of downtown Marigot. Most of the shops are closed until 9:30 a.m., so we have the brick and stone walkway to ourselves. We pass the Marigot Cemetery, as well as a Cigar shop, a swimwear store, a few restaurants and eventually come across a busy little neighborhood. There are locals standing in line at the Post office and kitty corner is a brightly orange painted bakery. The shop is busy. As people walk in, I also observe several people leave with long baguettes sticking out of brown paper bags. It's an unfamiliar sight to see so many people walking around with long loaves sticking out of their bags. My curiosity is peaked.

"Let's stop in…" Shanie and I say in unison and then laugh at this silly moment of a jinx.

We cross the narrow street and approach the open counter. I immediately admire all the bakery items, but my focus is locating those long baguettes. I quickly find them. There are several dozen cooling on stacked bakery racks a few feet behind the counters. Many of the trays have missing baguettes, which were probably all the ones I'd seen leaving the shop in paper bags.

Shanie is a pro at ordering at restaurants, so I ask her to purchase a few baguettes, and make my way to a little table located outside at the corner of the bakery. The table has two plastic white chairs and a bright red, orange, green and yellow stripped vinyl tablecloth.

It is easy to enjoy the island life that is on display at this little neighborhood shop. A tall, muscular Territorial Police Officer in pressed brown uniform stops in for a coffee and a roll. Two ladies are laughing and sipping coffee while minding their children who are busy drinking small juice boxes via straws. A businessman is on his cellphone chatting in French as one of the bakery workers brings him a second latte. He looks up to her and in mid-sentence from his phone conversations, says "Merci Beaucoup", and then seamlessly returns to his business call.

Shanie arrives with two small juices, a couple of six-inch sandwiches and two French baguettes. All on a bright orange cafeteria tray.

"Not bad for $10," she boasts.

"Really? I totally could get used to this lifestyle," I reply as the same bakery server who brought the business man's latte arrives with our coffees.

I grab one of the baguettes to see what all the fuss is about and after my first bite comprehend the seductive attraction. It is light and buttery with an even crisp crust. Easily one of the best baguettes I've ever tasted. I immediately tear off another big chunk and between hurried chews look across the table to my wife. She is sporting a black sun hat, black mini dress and black flip flops. Her smile and sheer enjoyment of her life during this café stop seems to emanate out of her soul.

We simply people watch for the next 20 or so minutes. It's a busy little section of Marigot. Opposite to the bakery is the Ebenezer Methodist church with its simple schoolhouse architecture and clean white fence. Across from the church is a short line of people for the post office. There is a steady stream of people coming and going in this area. It is an everyday morning in Marigot.

We pack up our belongings and Shanie leads me down the street. Strolling through the port city of Marigot is a bit like meandering through a small French village that had a fun marriage with the crowded randomness of unenforced building codes. The streets are narrow and lined with family-owned shops. You'll find everything from small convenience stores, to pharmacies, to small shops selling everything from pots and pans to backpacks and swimwear. It's all tightly packed together and many of the residents appear to live above their shops. There is laundry "air drying" in windows or clothes-pinned on laundry lines stretching across porch railings.

Shanie and I meander along Boulevard de France as shops open, proprietors sweep dirt and trash off their entrances. Several owners are raising their large protective metal gates that guard their storefronts.

We aren't in any particular hurry as we stroll to Super U, the largest market in Marigot. This French-owned grocery store is wonderfully stocked with exceptional French products including wine, cheese, meats, spreads as well as all the typical findings of a major grocery store.

The Super U is set back off Rue de Hollande, located across from a parking lot and the French sides-only McDonalds Restaurant. It is moderate in size compared to the mega grocery stores you'll find in most American cities. I grab a shopping cart as we pass through the automatic doors and like many of the shoppers here, Shanie and I will carry what we purchase. Unlike America, where so many people own large SUVs and feel the need to fill every inch of the cargo space, Shanie and I have to be diligent in contemplating what we need versus what we can carry.

We casually stroll through the aisles filling up our cart with bottled water, wine and other supplies for the day.

There are five checkout lines and uniquely, all of the checkers are seated near their conveyor belts. This creates an interesting dynamic between shopper and checker because they are always looking up to us for any interaction. The other odd note is that with all the checkers seated, the conveyer belts are relatively low. They only come to my mid-thigh. I ponder this set-up, taking it all in and only leave my day dream when I hear the lady pleasantly inquire, "euros or dollars?"

"Dollars would be great," I respond.

We place our items in the various bags we brought along and make our way back to Anse Des Sables for an afternoon of swimming and sunshine. For us, it is a day of "island life."

That evening as we sit on our little porch drinking a glass of wine, our thoughts are focused on each other and not a tropical storm named Irma somewhere of the coast of Africa.

EARLY WARNINGS

The blue sky is beckoning for everyone on the island to come out and play. To swim in calm turquoise waters, to lie upon soft white sand beaches and to soak up some healthy vitamin D from the magnificent tropical sun.

We start the day with our favorite pastime, coffee in bed. For us, nothing celebrates a new day better than the unmistakably, delicious and inviting aroma of freshly brewed coffee. It is our "morning mojo," our "let's get this day started," our "let's enjoy life elixir." The sun is peaking through the curtains and, for Shanie and I, all seems well with the world. That is until, we turn on CNN. The meteorologist is reporting that tropical Storm Irma has been upgraded to a hurricane and appears to be growing as it tracks west from the Cabo Verde Islands.

Overnight the wind speeds dramatically increased and are now gusting to 150 m.p.h. Irma is swirling between a Category 2 and Cat 3 Hurricane. The meteorologist reports while there is no definitive pathway, the Lesser Antilles islands should begin to keep a watch out for developments.

"Holy Shit," I turn to Shanie.

"Yeah, let's see what happens throughout the week."

"I don't know. This could be really dangerous," I add.

"We'll be careful, let's not get too excited yet," she replies, calming my nerves.

Shanie changes the subject to the possibilities of the morning. "Shall we go for baguettes and coffee this morning?"

"Absolutely." She coos snuggling back into her pillow while batting her eyes at me. The immediacy of the hurricane threat abates as we turn our attention to the enjoyment of our morning coffee and each other.

A few hours later we stroll our way to the Super U. To my surprise, there is no panic or frenzy in the grocery store. The store is not crowded and no one pushes, shoves or races through the aisles in hopes of getting their share of supplies. It's just another day on the island.

"I'm going to look for some batteries," as I leave the cart with my wife.

After a few unsuccessful attempts in different aisles, I finally find the battery section. I look over the shelves studying the various package amounts versus price when I notice a petit, middle-aged women also scouring the battery displays.

"Parlez vous, Englais?" I ask.

"Oui. Yes," she replies.

I introduce myself and steer the conversation to the reports of a hurricane possibly reaching the island. She too is concerned. As a charter boat captain, her boat is equipped with state-of-the-art weather and radar tracking instruments. She has been studying them and forecasts the hurricane could be very close to Saint Martin, if not directly over the island.

"Really?" I'm shocked.

"Yes, we are already taking precautions for our boat. We will position her in Simpson bay and attempt to web her together with other boats to help secure her."

"Wow, okay, thank you for the information. Umm, is it okay if I look you up after the storm? I would love to go on one of your charter cruises." I reply as I place some AA batteries in my cart.

She looks at me, like I haven't a clue in the world about hurricanes, which is true and says, "Au revoir. Bon Chance...and be careful," as she switches from French to English to better emphasize her warning.

I hustle to find Shanie and relay the new information from the boat captain. I cross over three aisles until I find her contemplating the various assortment of Nutella jars.

"Say hey, I just chatted with a sailboat captain and she is worried about the hurricane."

"What did she say?"

I tell her about the sailboat's weather equipment how her readings place the path of the hurricane close to the island, if not directly over it.

Shanie continues to look at Nutella jars, and after listening to the updated information places a medium sized jar into our cart turns to me and says, "Okay, let's keep an eye on the weather. We'll stop here every day and stock up on supplies."

"Okay, sounds good."

As we head to the bottled water section in the rear of the store. I proactively secure several more bottled waters before heading to the checkout lines.

I hand my credit card to the checker as Shanie and I pack our groceries into our backpacks and messenger bags.

We exit the store and immediately I can feel that the sleepy morning atmosphere of Marigot has transformed into the hustle and bustle of lunch time. Downtown Marigot is crowded with people moving up and down the sidewalks, cars clogging the narrow roadways. And the cacophony of the "one honk, two honks" system that locals use all over the island echoes throughout the small marine town.

One honk is to allow another car to enter traffic in front of you and two taps is a "Thank you."

Shanie and I enjoy our walk amongst the locals, but after several blocks carrying all the supplies, I suggest it's time for a cold Presidente.

She agrees and we stop at local bar on the corner of Rue de Holland and Rue F. Eboue. This is the type of place my wife and I love to seek out. It's totally local. A simple structure with a mis-matched corrugated steel roof, a small dining area with plastic tables and chairs, rusty metal fans tie-wired to the ceiling, and older upright beer coolers. One of the uprights is wrapped in a promotional message with an image of an ice-chilled Presi-dente as a small wave of ocean spray envelops the green bottle.

"Hello," I say to myself appreciating the cold beer advertise-ment.

The other cooler has a clear door front and a variety of beers resting on the shelves. After a quick scan of the bar I return my gaze to the Presidente-wrapped cooler and smile when I notice a hand-written note on the cooler.

"NO CREDIT. COME BACK TOMORROW...Thank you"

The note haphazardly taped with small chunks of black duct tape.

To the left of the upright coolers, just past some cases of beer, is an opening which leads to a small kitchen. The floors and walls are lined with white square tiles. It looks clean compared to the wood and dirt floors of the dining area. I watch a lady in a red t-shirt and blue jean shorts hurriedly go back and forth from the food prep area to what I assume are the skillets located behind the wall of the upright beer coolers.

An older man, who could be the husband of the cook, steps over from tending to another customer at the bar takes my order.

"Two Presidentes, s'l vous plait," I ask as I dig out some cash from my pocket, knowing they will not be taking any credit cards today.

The gentleman pulls out two cold beers, pops the tops and places them on the bar for me.

"$3.00," he smiles at me.

"Merci, merci," as I hand him a five, "keep the change." I then turn to take the wonderfully chilled bottles to Shanie who is seated at one of the rickety tables.

"I love it here."

"I love it to," she says winking at me.

"Cheers," as we clink our beers, which I quickly guzzle.

"Ahhh, let's have another?"

"Hello! Of course!" Shanie bursts out and then drains hers.

I return to the bar and order a couple more beers as Shanie finds her way to the unisex bathroom.

I look around and admire the simplicity of the bar, kitchen and loosely organized tables. It's comfortable, friendly and best of all, local.

"Let's head back and swim this aft?" I suggest as Shanie returns to the table.

"I'll watch you swim and hang out on the beach and read," she replies.

After we enjoy our beers, we thank the bartender and optimistically say we'll stop in after the hurricane. He nods affirmatively. I gather up our groceries and we take a leisurely stroll back to Anse Des Sables.

After a great afternoon of snorkeling and sunbathing we decide it is the perfect evening to have dinner at one of the restaurants located in the Marina Royale District.

The district is as picturesque as it sounds and is designed in a U-shape configuration. Several fine French restaurants line the lagoon which places diners merely feet from million-dollar catamarans that are docked directly in front of the various restaurants.

Shanie and I walk the floating piers that separate the boats from the restaurants and after reviewing the "Le Galion" nightly specials decide this is the perfect spot. Tonight's specials, beautifully handwritten in chalk on the dockside sandwich board includes Lobster Crepe, Mahi Tartare, Whole Red Snapper or always my favorite, the Butcher Plate which is a cornucopia of Flank Steak, Spicy Sausage, Chicken and Pork Tenderloin.

The host tells us to find a table we would like. The place isn't overly busy, and we notice three Gendarmes in full uniform enjoying dinner at a table close to the bar. It's nice to see their presence on the island. Shanie and I scan the available tables and quickly decide to take the open table close to where a 46-foot catamaran is tethered to large cement posts of the dock. The beautiful catamaran is about ten feet from us and we can easily look into the living area and galley of this magnificent boat.

As we take our seats, Shanie notices a waiter from one of the restaurants in Marigot, L'Arawak, which is named after the Indian tribe that originally inhabited the island. Jean-Michelle is a renowned local character full of energy and unique fashion sense. Looking at him you would swear he has the same DNA as workout guru Richard Simmons. Unique to Jean-Michelle is his choice of wardrobe. He always wears an old-school cotton tennis headband which color coordinates with whatever shirt he has on. He is having dinner with a date and as they stand up to greet us, Shanie and I are both shocked to see she towers over him and is easily six feet tall. She completely dwarfs Jean-Michelle. With the dramatic height difference and his purple headband and purple T-shirt they are quite the spectacle at this quaint harbor restaurant.

We quickly order a bottle of Cotes du Rhone and, after the waiter pours us a glass, we share a toast with Jean-Michelle and his Amazonian girlfriend. We salute to the joy of the evening and to the hopes the storm spares the island.

One of the real treasures of Saint Martin is the professional French chefs that oversee the kitchens. Most are schooled in Paris and their skills are legendary. Shanie and I order our meals and, while we dine on this wonderful French cuisine, discuss tomorrow's adventure. The plan is to scope out a condo for sale which overlooks the Marina. The condo is listed at $90,000, which we find affordable considering it is on the top floor, comes with two decks with million-dollar views of the Marina Royale harbor. We finish off our meals with two West Indies coffees and then take a leisurely stroll along the marina back to our place at Anse de Sable. It is our honeymoon and for a second night, completely immerse in the harmony of love and togetherness.

HURRICANE PREPARATION LIST

I've just reviewed the update from the National Oceanic and Atmospheric Administration (NOAA), which now projects that Irma has the potential to grow into one of the largest hurricanes of the season and advises all listeners to take necessary measures.

"Wow, this could get very real. I think we should get more supplies to ride out the storm."

"I agree. We'll head back to the Super U this morning," Shanie offers between sips of coffee.

My wife is the daughter of a Navy Commander and decorated A6 Jet Pilot who flew over 41 sorties in Vietnam. Her father attributed his survival to three things. 1. Always prepare by reviewing a myriad of "What if" scenarios. 2. Don't let someone else's mistake kill you. 3. Luck helps.

Shanie is a product of this military upbringing and to her credit, adopted all of these teachings, especially preparing "What if" scenarios.

She grabs our laptop and quickly searches the web for hurricane prep lists. Within moments she has compiled a list for our shopping trip.

> Mosquito repellent
> Sun Block
> Bleach

Antiseptic spray/band aids/first aid kit
Bottle water
Food supplies to last at least 7 days, including
Ramen noodles
Cans of ravioli
Cans of tuna or chicken
Can Opener
Candles
Matches/lighters
Large Garbage/Leaf bags
A can of Sterno or charcoal briquettes

Her research also advises to freeze large water bottles. If you lose power, you can move a few of the frozen bottles to the refrigerator and prolong the life of perishables. It's also a good idea to freeze baguettes to preserve their freshness.

Her research also suggested we fill all available pails or buckets with drinking water and some with pool water to help flush toilets. Equally important is to top off all propane tanks and your car's fuel tank.

"How about another cup of coffee and then we'll head into town?" She asks with her cup extended my way. This is my wife's loving gesture for me to "pretty please" make her another cup.

We make our way to the Super U and easily gather most everything on her hurricane pre-list. There is plenty of stock at the grocery store, and there has been no rush on hurricane supplies. Because we have so many more items on this trip, we opt to catch a taxi to help us bring it all back to the condo. It's easy to catch a taxi on the island and, after a quick ride back to the condo, we sort and organize our supplies.

Although we are concerned about the approaching hurricane, the atmosphere of the island is still calm. So, we decide to still take a look at the property at Marina Royale. On one of her previous trips to the island, Shanie had befriended a real estate agent named Bruno. He works out of a small office next to a coffee shop situated just across the way from the Marina Royale District. We have a 1:00 p.m. meeting and his place of work is only a short walk from Anse De Sables.

We easily find Bruno's office where he's sitting at his desk. As soon as he sees Shanie he pops up out of his chair and greets her with a warm embrace. He then extends a long arm to me for introductions.

Bruno is immediately likeable and seems to embody the islands marketing slogan, "The Friendly Island." The conversation between us is easy as we enjoy the short walk to view the property for sale. We stroll across Rue de Kennedy and enter the Royale Marine district. As you enter Royale Marine from the street, the walkway guides you through various restaurants. We walk past open kitchens, stock rooms and utility closets. It all seems uniquely "island" to me as we watch the various chefs and restaurant employees prepping for tonight's dinner menus.

We make our way to the front of the restaurant and the pier that borders the Marina. The marina is also home to several jewelry and clothing shops as well as the various restaurants and cafes. Above the many businesses are residential condos with wonderful patios and decks that overlook the marina. It all has charm and character until we approach the entrance to the condo complex where the listing is located. All the quaintness and appeal is replaced by an unsettling government housing ambiance that emanates from the building. The heavy iron security door and bleak brick and dilapidated entryway make me think this place is more like a drug den than an island condominium paradise. I begin to understand the moderate listing price.

Bruno is unfazed by the condition of the entryway and guides us through the gate and up three flights of stairs. At the landing, we take a left and walk down a long hallway with all different types of doors and security latches. Each door is a different color and type of wood. It all looks haphazard. I exhale in frustration, because I can only imagine what the inside of the condo looks like after entering the building and walking past all these mismatched doors. At the end of the hall, we make a left turn and continue down a short hallway that has only three doors. Bruno opens the first door on the left and immediately bright sunny daylight floods into the hallway.

"Wow. What a view!" Shanie exclaims as she lowers her sunglasses and steps into the condo.

To my utter dismay, the unit is big, bright with lots of glass, a bedroom loft upstairs and two decks that overlook the shops and harbor. The panorama is stunning. The view is wonderful, the condition of the condo is not.

It looks as if the previous owners left the place halfway through their move out. There are clothes and garbage scattered throughout the main living area. There is bedding, chairs, a worn-out washing machine on the deck. I look under the large wooden table in the living room to find an egg carton with a remaining half dozen eggs.

"I'm not going to touch that," I say to both Bruno and Shanie. This causes us all to laugh and we agree best to leave the mysterious egg carton alone.

We take our time and open the dilapidated cupboards and drawers and find partial sets of dishware and cutlery. All the cabinets would have to be replaced in the kitchen and both bathrooms, but the flooring looks okay. We head upstairs to the loft and find it to also be uncared for and abandoned. But the view from the upper deck is spectacular.

As Bruno heads back downstairs from the loft, Shanie and I hang back to confer about the condo.

"Maybe offer $70,000? The view is amazing, but this place needs at least $15,000 in repairs."

"Yeah, wow, but we could make it work. You love these types of projects and maybe the buyer is motivated. Let's talk to Bruno about it," Shanie confers.

Bruno suggests we head to the Le Galion Restaurant, grab some cold Presidentes and chat about our next steps.

"Yes, please!" I quickly respond as we head out of the condo.

The restaurant is steps from the condo and Shanie and I are pleasantly surprised to have the same waiter from the previous night.

After the beers arrive, we toast to Bruno and discuss our offer.

"It needs a lot of work to make it habitable," I say to Bruno.

"But the potential is great," Shanie chimes in.

"We'd like to put in an offer of $70,000," I tell him.

"Okay, I'm not sure the owner will accept that, but I'm happy to make it for you on your behalf," Bruno answers as we celebrate with another "Salute."

I look up to the waiter at the bar, raise my beer and with my other hand signal for three more.

The waiter brings us the beers and the conversation at the table turns to the approaching hurricane. Bruno has lived through hurricanes before and, while cautious about the approaching storm, doesn't seem overly concerned.

"It's the island way," he adds.

"Hurricanes come and go, be ready, but it is the price you have to pay to live in paradise. And if you become a property owner here, you'll learn that."

"I hope you're right. I'm more than a little bit worried about it, myself," I reply.

"Well, the good thing about the unit you want is that the management has just replaced all the roofs."

"Well, we have that going for us!" I respond as we toast again.

The waiter comes over and I ask for the tab. As we leave the restaurant, Shanie and I pause to take it all in. We have just placed an offer on a condo, have a great real estate agent, and the process has begun to create a second home in Saint Martin. All seems fine with the world. Even the hurricane reports are not as dire as earlier reported. The island is paradise and a false sense of calm seems to have gripped everyone. Including Shanie and me.

SUNDAY BEST

The French side has a deep religious history and most every Sunday locals attend services at one of the many quaint neighborhood churches. Shanie and I are drinking cappuccinos and enjoying baguettes at our favorite bakery, which is kitty corner to one of these small churches. The lovely sound of the church bells draws our attention as the arched doors of the Ebenezer Methodist Church swing open.

In an orderly and joyous manner, the attendees seem to be "on parade" as they exit. Everyone is impeccably dressed. The men in sport jackets with crisp white shirts and the women in colorful dresses with complementary colored pumps.

As soon as many of the women step outside, they pause to open their parasols to shade themselves from the sun before continuing with their families down the few church steps. Everyone chats as they queue past the minister who stands by the open doors. It appears he is thanking each and every church member for attending the day's service. It is a beautiful blue-sky day and the combination of neighborly friendliness, bright dresses, multi-colored parasols and the crisp white shirts, makes the whole setting look like a scene from a 1950s film.

Shanie and I are mesmerized watching the procession. None of the church members are in a hurry or seem concerned about the approaching storm. Several families slowly stroll across the street to purchase drinks and sandwiches from the bakery. There is a casual ambiance to the entire scene as we listen to the laughter and playful screams of the local children who dash about us. Many of the smaller kids now clumsily carry baguettes almost as big as them.

We finish up our drinks and store our baguettes and ham sandwiches in my backpack. Our next plan is to again make our way back to the Super U for yet more supplies. The morning weather update relayed that Irma is fluctuating between category 2 and category 3 with winds up to 115 mph. The announcer explained it was difficult to predict its exact path due to the "Bermuda High." This weather phenomenon is a high-pressure zone that would prevent the hurricane from tracking in a more northerly route.

Irma is moving along the bottom portion of this high-pressure zone and they can't seem to predict how long the Bermuda High will hold. Apparently, it interacts with the jet stream from the Pacific Ocean that flows east across the United States, and if at any time the Bermuda High shifts northward it will force the hurricane to follow suit, and greatly alter its progression through the Caribbean, perhaps missing many of the islands as it heads north into the Atlantic Ocean. What this all means to Shanie and I, and perhaps many of the locals on the island, is that no one knows how close Irma will pass by the island, let alone travel directly over it.

As we stroll along one of the sidewalks, we cross over to another block to walk by a section of wall that is magnificently aged and distressed with wide stripes of tan and aqua blue.

"We have to take a selfie against this wall. It's amazing!" I urge Shanie.

She is wearing her black sun hat and a striking black and white sun dress with bright yellow trim. I assure her it will pop out against the distressed wall. We take two selfies. The first is a typical selfie with big smiles. In the second photo, as a joke, we give our best hurricane panicked expressions.

"Well, hopefully we won't have to use this one if the hurricane comes," she says, smiling as she flicks back and forth between the two photos on my cellphone.

As we make our way into the Super U, we are again surprised that it is not crowded with panicked islanders arming themselves with supplies. It's eerily calm inside the store. Shanie and I easily find the few remaining items on our list, and we move effortlessly through checkout. We pack the supplies into a couple of backpacks and decide to make our way to one of Shanie's favorite restaurants in Marigot. L'Arhawak. The restaurant is situated in the heart of downtown Marigot. It's a street-side restaurant open on three sides and centered around a giant tree that shoots up through a green canvas tarp that shades most of the dining tables. The kitchen area is hidden inside a building behind all the tables. There is a mobile bar that rests on large wheels. This is so it can be rolled close to the street to entice shoppers to step over the curb and sit on a comfortable bar stool in the shade. It also allows the bar to be rolled back towards the building if the nearby Caribbean Sea overflows the banks and floods the downtown area. Apparently, this occurs often during hurricanes.

The restaurant is a wonderful spot to people watch while sipping on cold Presidentes or French Rose. Jean-Michelle, the Richard Simmons doppelganger, is working the tables and is excited to see us. He quickly sits us at one of the best tables.

Jean-Michelle takes our drink orders and returns with our ice-cold drinks while we peruse the menu. Shanie loves their French Onion Soup and I opt for the chicken kabobs. Jean-Michelle informs us that most of the restaurants in town will close, tomorrow, as they shutter things and prepare for whatever storm may be on its way. He doesn't appear to be overly concerned as he brings us another round of drinks.

We are in no hurry and enjoy the local scene unfolding around us. There is an old man strolling with a horse and he frequently stops to let children pet his horse. The parrot riding atop the saddle only adds to the spectacle. Our meals arrive and I am again stunned by the quality of the food. For something as simple as Chicken Kabobs, this French Chef has done something magical to them. They are moist, tender, perfectly seasoned and served piping hot. Shanie's French Onion Soup is definitely a meal in itself. While sipping Rosé, she describes how the soup is prepared over several days; knowledge she acquired from her earlier visit in June.

After finishing our meal and a round of drinks courtesy of Jean-Michelle, we say our good-byes and walk towards the water's edge and stare west across the beautiful Caribbean. A short distance from where we stand, the city of Marigot erected an ideal photo sculpture. "I ❤ SXM." SXM is the airport code for the island and both the French and Dutch sides have adopted it as one of the favorite ways to market their island.

A family of four is trying to take some pictures next to this landmark, so Shanie and I offer to help. After several attempts to get the young kids and parents all looking in the same direction, we are able to capture some wonderful pictures. I hand the phone back to the father and wish them luck over the next several days. Shanie and I then continue our leisurely stroll, hand-in-hand back to our condo at Anse Des Sables.

The streets aren't busy as we pass Le Beach hotel and stroll through the parking lot, as a few guests unload supplies and carry them into the hotel.

We make our way to our condo and after we unpack our supplies, I offer my wife a glass of wine.

I hand her a glass as I take mine to the couch and log onto the WIFI with my phone. There is an urgent message from my father-in-law. It terrifies me.

Billy and Shanie,

TRIED TO CALL YOU TODAY TO TALK ABOUT THE STORM AND GET THE ADDRESS, PERSON'S NAME, AND PHONE NUMBER WHERE YOU MAY MOVE.

IT IS TIME TO PREPARE FOR THE WORSE POSSIBLE. I TRUST THE EURO MODEL THAT NOW HAS THE EYE MOVING OVER YOUR ISLAND;
AND THE SPAGHETTI MODELS THAT HAD THE STORM PASSING NORTH OF YOU 24 HRS AGO NOW HAVE THE STORM PASSING OVER YOU.

OF COURSE NO ONE KNOWS EXACTLY WHERE IRMA WILL TRACK BUT BEST TO BE PREPARED, A CAT 4 IS POSSIBLE. CATASTROPHIC DAMAGE DUE TO HIGH STORM SURGE, TORRENTIAL RAIN, AND 125 PLUS WINDS.

THE MARINE DATA COMING IN SHOWS THAT IRMA MAY GROW INTO A CAT 5 PLUS HURRICANE. ONE PREDICTIVE SITE IS SHOWING MONSTER WAVES 52 FEET TALL WITH 16 SEC INTERVALS AND WINDS OF 191 MPH.

AS YOU CAN IMAGINE THE EAST COAST AND GULF STATES ARE STARTING TO PAY ATTENTION.

IF YOU CAN GET ON YOU TUBE THERE ARE GOOD METEOROLOGIST SHOWING THE DATA AND MODELS WITH EXCELLENT EXPLANATIONS.

STAY SAFE!
WE LOVE YOU, MADDY SAYS HI.

ROD & PATTI

"Fuck," I say to Shanie as I pass my phone over to her.

After reading his email. I'm afraid for myself. I'm afraid for

Billy Nahn

Shanie. I'm afraid for the entire island.

A NIGHTMARE & OUR FIRST EVACUATION

T he hurricane reports are getting more and more dire. The cyclone is intensifying and growing in size. The trajectory predictions, although varied, show her traveling close to or directly over Saint Martin. There are two international models for tracking hurricanes. The USA model and the European model. The slight difference is the algorithms of the USA model use less data, so the reports can be updated more rapidly. The European model, albeit more accurate, takes longer for the computers to analyze because of all the different data streams. Both models agree on the size of the storm and her growing ferocity. All the spaghetti strings representing the possible paths for the hurricane from the various models are actually tightly packed with her barreling directly for Saint Martin.

Shanie and I have downloaded a few hurricane apps for our iPhones. The NHC (National Hurricane Center) becomes a key information source for us. They provide regular updates at three-hour increments. We also start to follow the NOAA (National Oceanic and Atmospheric Administration) page on Facebook. The other information source I have is my father-in-law, Rod Bankson. He is emailing me constant updates but, like his previous email, has an old military habit of writing all the emails in capital letters. For whatever reason, I feel like he is shouting at me from the United States and I have a hard time focusing on his steady delivery of emails. After about six of them, each one in all capital letters, the best I can mentally handle is to quickly scan them. But to his credit, his information completely confirms what I'm learning from the NCH and NOAA.

Our condo owner, Estelle is also in contact with us regarding Irma. She wants us to relocate to another unit. This unit is located on the ground floor and would be on the street side or garden side of the Anse Des Sables complex. Estelle's plan involves her mother coming by around 4:00 p.m. to help us pack up our belongings and move everything to the ground level condo. Her cogent thinking is that most often in hurricanes, the roof is the first to suffer catastrophic damage. If we were to stay on the third level, and the roof gets sheared off, our ability to safely find refuge would be extremely difficult if not fatal. It's logical, but this plan does not sit well with me.

Anse Des Sables is located along the shore of the Caribbean Sea and even a slight rise in sea levels could bring catastrophic flooding. After Hurricanes Katrina and Harvey and the perils of storm surge, being on the ground floor scares me.

Irma is churning into a massive storm and I can vividly imagine a wall of storm surge blasting through our complex; possibly drowning us as well as every other resident on the ground floor.

Shanie and I discuss several options and agree we need to consider possible "What if?" scenarios. After a few glasses of wine, we are exhausted and decide to turn in.

"Let's think about our plans in the a.m." Shanie reassures me as she drifts off.

But I am semi-awake, tossing and turning. It's now about 2:00 a.m. and I reach for my phone to check the latest updates from the National Hurricane Center (NHC). It's more of the same about Irma. She is coming for us and growing along the way. I cuddle next to Shanie. She embraces me, which slows my breathing and I too finally nod off.

At some point, I begin to dream. I'm not sure what is happening at the onset of the dream, but everything else that follows is a nightmare. It's a crystal clear vision of me floating over a body lying face down in the sand. I float there for a while, looking over the beach area and colorless water. I then reach down to the body, and surprisingly, it is easy to turn over. To my complete shock, what I am looking at is myself. It's my body that has drowned.

I call out and am instantly catapulted from my horrifying dream world to the real world. I lie in the dark for a long, long time as I try to slow my pulse and mull over what limited options I have to better ensure the safety of Shanie and myself.

I decide that the dream sequence is prophecy. Shanie and I cannot stay in Anse Des Sables. We must find a way off the island or find other, safer accommodations. As daylight creeps in under the patio curtains, I sit up in bed and start staring at my wife while she sleeps. It's like I'm in a trance. She finally rolls over, stretches and blinks several times as she gently awakens. Once her eyes adjust to the light level in the room, she realizes I am staring at her.

"Whoa, what is it honey?" she asks.

"There is no way in hell we are going to relocate to the first-floor condo," I spurt out. I then give her a detailed retelling of my nightmare.

To her credit, she doesn't question or attempt to dispel my emotions. She stretches her legs, swings them over to the floor and gets out of bed

"Okay," she says. "Let's make some calls."

"I'll try and get us a flight." Motivated by her responsive and supportive actions.

It doesn't take long for me to realize we've waited too long to look for flights off the island. I cannot find a single available seat on any of the major USA airlines. Everything is sold out. Additionally, Princess Juliana International Airport is expecting to close at noon tomorrow in anticipation of the hurricane's arrival later that night.

I'm as desperate as I've ever been in my half century, so I don't give up and keep looking for a flight to escape this island. I do a Google search for other airlines flying into and out of Saint Martin and come across Copa Airlines. I've never heard of this airline, but their website informs me they are part of the Star Alliance. I am hopeful.

It's 7:00 a.m. and, while I search for flights on Copa Airlines, Shanie between sips of her coffee, sends a text to a couple she met on a previous visit to the island; Alain and Martine Pages. In April, they purchased Villa Haiku, an Indonesian-styled Bed and Breakfast villa. It's located on the opposite side of Marigot in the upper north east corner of the island near Orient Bay. Their home is nestled on one of the highest points in an exclusive area called Les Jardins Des Orient Bay. Shanie has spoken highly of them from the very minute she returned from the island back in June. She even played a drone video Alain made showing all the buildings of their property. She really liked this couple and had met them at the Bikini Bar in Orient Beach. They shared cocktails, danced to a local band and the next day she visited their retreat.

I locate a number for Copa Airlines and speak to a nice ticket agent. I have a hard time understanding his English but am grateful this might lead to a plane ride off the island. He informs me they have a flight leaving tomorrow for Panama City at 12:25 p.m. and the cost is about $900 per ticket.

"I'll take those two seats," I tell him without a moment's hesitation.

"Okay, let me get your name and email address," he politely responds.

For the next 20 minutes, we go back and forth trying to clarify the spellings of our names, our birthdates and email addresses. I have zero confidence any of the information the agent has written down is correct. I also find it extremely odd that he does not want my credit card number to secure the seats or provide me with a ticket locater number.

"You can pay for the tickets when you check in to the airport," he reassures me.

I've never worked with Copa Airlines, so while I am skeptical, I go along with his explanation of the process. And I know the airport is closing at noon and yet this flight is scheduled to take off at 12:25 p.m. But the agent, is not concerned at all about it. After about another 15 or so minutes I hang up the phone and look at Shanie. She is looking at me and shakes her head. After overhearing much of this conversation with the ticket agent, she too understands the likelihood we do not have any reserved seats on that plane leaving the island.

After another cup of coffee, Shanie starts to pack up our clothes and organize all our hurricane supplies. She is laying things out on top of the condo's king-size bed. She has made seven or eight neat piles each containing various items. One pile has our candles, batteries, matches, lighters and my flashlight. Another pile consists of the many dry goods we had hauled from the Super U grocery store in Marigot. Several multi-packs of ramen noodles, 4 boxes of crackers and several baguettes. Another pile consists of Nutella, jelly and peanut butter. She also has a pile with all our medicines, bug spray and antiseptic washes. Our alcohol pile consists of a 5-liter box of Chateau Bordeaux, 3-liter box of Rosé and a 4-Liter box of Merlot. Shanie also brings out the 30, 2-liter water bottles we had stocked piled. With all our supplies somewhat coordinated she turns to start organizing her suitcase.

I keep trying in vain to locate my tickets on the Copa Airlines' website. But my searches come up fruitless. I can't find any re-assurance we have tickets. Several times I try my last name, and then Shanie's last name, nothing is bringing up a ticket locator number or indication we have seats on a flight.

As I get more and more frustrated with the airline, Shanie's phone dings signifying a text message. It is from Martine. I look at her and wait while she reads the text. Shanie is poker faced and has a habit of never talking while reading texts, so I have to wait for what seems like an eternity to find out what it reads.

"It's from Martine, and says we are welcome to ride the hurri-cane out at Villa Haiku." Shanie smiles at me seeing the sheer re-lief on my face.

"But, Martine wants to know if we can go to the hardware store and find a propane gas camping stove," she adds.

"Okay, let me see what I can do about finding a stove."

Although, I have been on the island for about a week, I am un-familiar with neighborhoods outside the immediate vicinity of our condo. But as I look on my phone's GPS it appears there is a Home'N Tools store nearby located somewhere on the other side of the Marina Royale district. I try and memorize the map because I don't have cellular service on my phone. I grab my wallet and tell Shanie I'm off to try and find us that stove.

She says she will consolidate our luggage and pack only what we might need for the next couple days and that we'll leave every-thing else in the condo. Both of us naively thinking we'll prob-ably return by the weekend.

I walk down the two flights of stairs to the ground floor and im-mediately feel the heat of the day. As I open the double doors to the walkway that leads past the pool to the security gate of the complex and street, a sense of serious urgency has gripped the island. The roadway is clogged with traffic. People are hurrying in all directions carrying waters and bags of supplies. The "Le Beach Hotel" parking lot is jammed with coming and going as guests unload provisions from their trunks and quickly head into the hotel.

I try to use my phone's GPS to get my bearing and generally locate the Home'N Tools store. My phone is useless because I don't have a local SIM Card and for whatever reason, I could never get on AT&T's international plan. In the upper left corner where it normally reads five circles and the words "AT&T," it reads "No Service."

The cars, trucks and mopeds continually scurry up and down Rue de Sandy Ground as I desperately try to hail a taxi. Before today, it was a simple process. While there are no yellow cabs or corporate branded cabs, you locate taxis by looking at the license plates. Each cab's license plate consists of a series of numbers followed by the word "TAXI." I see no available taxis. After walking about 2 blocks up the street towards downtown Marigot, I decide to turn around and walk back, still trying to wave down a taxi. I walk past our condo, the laundry shop and continue along the road towards the Sandy Ground area. This is all new territory to me, and all I see are more cars and racing mopeds.

Feeling lost, I return to the condo. I'm helpless without a taxi so I just start to wave at every van or car in hopes that perhaps someone will just pull over and give me a ride. After a several failed attempts, a rather beat up van pulls into the parking lot across the condo near the soccer field and waves to me. I hurriedly cross the street, open the sliding van door and say, "thanks." The inside of the van is dirty, disorganized and smells of mildew. The driver doesn't say a word.

"Home'N Tools?" I ask.

He nods and pulls out of the parking lot into traffic.

"Is it far?"

Again, silence from the driver, but meekly points in the direction we are headed. We drive past the Marigot Cemetery and then take a right onto Rue de President Kennedy. It's a totally uncomfortable situation. I have no idea where he is going and feel trapped and unsafe.

"Arrêtez. Arrêtez" I frantically shout.

He slams the brakes, lurching me forward and points in the direction he was heading and shouts something in a language I've never heard. Frustrated and worried, I pull out a $10 bill, shove it into his hand and jump out of the van. I hurry across the street to get away from the van and walk towards a pharmacy. A young man with a pony tail walks down the steps.

"Pardon moi, parlez vous englais?"

He nods back and forth and replies, "A little."

I ask him directions to the Home'N Tools store and if I can walk there. "Non, non, too far."

"Merci, merci," I say to him, and after a deep breath, decide the best decision might be to head back to our condo and worry later about the propane stove.

The sidewalks are overfilling with people carrying bottled waters and bags of groceries. It's as if the whole town just woke up this morning and realized there is a massive hurricane approaching.

"Where were you all this week and what were you doing?" I think out loud.

I'm waiting for a break in the traffic to cross the street and realize my escape from the taxi has given me a lift in energy. I move quickly past some shops and past the Marina. As I walk along the Marigot cemetery I start looking at license plates for taxis. The streets are jammed with cars in both lanes and the constant honking of horns adds to the tension. I see a newer van pass in the direction of our condo and instinctively wave to it. The lady's eyes dart up to her rearview mirror and then she looks over her shoulder back to me. But, unfortunately keeps driving on. I get to within a block of the condo and I recognize the van. By the grace of something larger than myself...the earth...or the universe, this lady has pulled into the same soccer parking lot as the other driver; and is patiently waiting for me. She waves for me to come over. As I slide her van door open, she greets me with a hearty laugh and smile.

"I saw you and figured you needed something," she says in perfect English.

I almost reach out to pinch her to see if she is real. Her name is Joyce and she is an independent taxi driver. Her new taxi is spotless and the air conditioning provides instant relief. Joyce radiates goodness and happiness from the driver's seat. With her accent and striking looks she may have a Jamaican heritage mixed with some local French upbringing. Whatever her ancestry, it is a wondrous blend. I notice several gold rings as she hands me her business card and delightfully inquires, "Where to?"

"Home'N Tools."

"No problem." She laughs again pulling into traffic. Joyce is chatty and I ask her if she would mind waiting for me in the store as I just need to purchase a few items. She laughs, and says "Of course, no problem."

I lean back into the bench seat and take a deep breath. After a short drive around the backside of the Marina Royale and up a snaking hill we see the large parking lot for the Home'N Tools store. There are two Gendarmes directing traffic. Joyce pulls right up to the front of the store, like she owns it, and tells me to jump out. She lets me know she will circle the lot and wait.

55

I'm just stupefied by her sunshine, energy and go-get-it-done attitude. An angel driving a taxi on the island of Saint Martin.

The hardware store is crowded and busy, but less the sense of panic than on the streets. The staff are dressed in easy-to-spot red polo shirts and people are patient while they wait for help. A young mother with a child in her arms asks a female staff member where to find weatherproofing silicone. When they finish, she turns to me and I ask about camping stoves. She shakes her head. "Those have been sold out for a few days, now. Sorry."

"Okay. Thanks for your help."

After a quick look down several aisles not seeing anything we might need, I exit the store and look for Joyce's van. She has found a little parking spot near the Gendarmes and is checking her cell phone as I climb in.

"No luck, but thanks for waiting."

"Sorry about that, where to now?" she asks.

"Anse des Sables, but we are relocating... I have no idea where we are going. But, my wife will know? Can you wait for us to load up our supplies and take us there

"Sure, no problem." She responds with a smile.

There is a makeshift bus stop in front of our condo that no one has ever used for that dedicated purpose. In fact, over the past few days, a moped was locked up inside the bus stop. Today, it is vacant, so Joyce simply pulls right up into the bus stop and parks. Before I exit the van, I hand her $25 dollars for the ride and for waiting for us.

"We have many, many bags and it will take several trips to load them all," I tell her.

She unlocks her seatbelt, grabs some cigarettes out of her purse and exits the driver's door. As she lights her cigarette, she laughs and says, "No problem, I'll be right here."

I race up the path past the pool and the three flights of stairs to our condo. The door is open.

"Hey Babe. Holy fuck, you would not believe what just happened," I shout entering the condo.

I give her a quick recap of my travails and let her know we have the most incredible taxi driver waiting outside to give us a ride to Villa Haiku.

"Jesus. Thank goodness you're safe."

"It's a fucking zoo out there!" I add, looking over all the work she has done prepping our supplies. Everything is organized into an assortment of hand bags, grocery bags and garbage bags for transporting.

"Well, we're pretty set here so you can start loading her van," she confidently tells me.

After several trips between the condo and the taxi, with Joyce helping us arrange our bags, we are ready to depart.

Joyce closes the hatch as Shanie jumps into the front passenger seat and describes the general direction to Villa Haiku. Joyce seems familiar with the neighborhood and laughs, saying, "No problem."

My wife promptly goes into full conversation mode, like she did with our Uber driver, which now totally seems like a lifetime ago. She uncovers that Joyce has been to the USA several times and, most recently, for a shopping trip to LA. They discuss how affordable clothing is in America compared to the island. I stare out the window towards the Caribbean Sea. I see a few sailboats heading into the harbor, the water and sky looking like a picture from a postcard. Not even a hint of any bad weather heading our way.

"I just have to say..." I interrupt their discussion about LA and shopping, "...the first three letters of your name "Joyce," spell 'Joy' and that is what I feel right now. I can't thank you enough for all your help."

Joyce and Shanie both laugh at this comment, which doesn't bother me at all. For the first time since my frightening nightmare, I feel confident in the actions we are undertaking.

The roads are very crowded with cars, trucks, mopeds and people carrying bottled waters. We drive past, the L'Arhawak restaurant and the Care Maritime Ferry building and make a right turn to a large roundabout that gets us onto the Route de Nationale #7(N7); the roadway that circles the island.

Shanie and Joyce discuss trying to purchase some funeral candles. These long cylindrical candles last for over twenty hours and the glass casing protects the flame. We pause at another roundabout and discuss buying these candles at the Super U. Joyce looks at the queue of traffic that has now stalled. There is a line of cars bleeding out into this roadway as they wait to fill their fuel tanks. Joyce makes a quick decision to abort going to the Super U, steps on the gas, snakes between two cars and drives north up the N7.

"There are several smaller, local markets on the way. We'll stop at one of those," she confirms.

"Joyce, have you had any time to get supplies?" Shanie asks.

"No, I've been working, but I'll get to it."

This surprises both Shanie and me. I wonder if Joyce has any regrets about not getting supplies, especially after seeing how much we had purchased and loaded into her van. After six years of a close marriage, Shanie and I have developed the ability to simply look at each other and communicate via eye brow raises, questioning stares and simple hand gestures. Shanie looks at me and tilts her head, and without saying anything, I understand her desire to help purchase some supplies for Joyce.

I nod and smile in silent confirmation.

Joyce drives us up a long hill towards the town of Grand Case. This is my first real glimpse of the less affluent neighborhoods of Saint Martin. We are driving through an area that looks much more third world than first. Many of the homes appear neglected and in various states of disrepair. Also surprising is how close they are to the N7. In some sections they are just feet from the road. I am more than a little taken aback by this new dilapidated landscape compared to the vacationer's veneer of turquoise waters, champagne restaurants and the upscale marinas.

Joyce puts on her left turn signal to pull into a local convenience mart. The entranceway is steep and there is a steady line of cars heading in the opposite direction blocking our way into the parking lot. An old man sitting on a wall by the driveway gets up and without any hesitation walks directly into traffic and holds up his arms to halt the oncoming traffic. This provides Joyce with an opening to make her left turn into the parking lot. The old man returns to his seat as Joyce and Shanie get out of the van and head into the store. Joyce says something in French to the old man who smiles and goes back to watching the traffic. Before exiting the taxi, Joyce asks me to please stay in the van. My guess is to keep any eye on our supplies as well as protect her brand-new taxi.

From my vantage point, I watch the entrance to the convenience mart and the checkout counter located just inside the door. I observe Shanie and Joyce load up with baguettes, waters, a bag of charcoal briquettes and several funeral candles. There is no sense of panic at the mart and the checker bags the different items, separating my wife and Joyce's purchases. As they leave the store, I exit the van and open the back hatch to help load the supplies. Shanie quietly mentions that she bought Joyce several waters, but unfortunately, that is all she would accept.

"Oh really? I was hoping we could get more for her," I reply, closing the back hatch.

"Yes, me too," Shanie adds.

At the sound of the van's ignition, the old man rises from his perch and walks again into two-lane traffic. Joyce backs down the steep pitch and across the southbound traffic lane, stepping on the gas pedal to get us into the flow of traffic. She rolls down her window, honks and waves to the kind man who helped us.

We continue our journey to Villa Haiku. The narrow tree-lined road leads us past quaint inns, small residential enclaves and other specialty shops and businesses. It is idyllic and yet totally different than the west side of the island and the city of Marigot. After a few more twists and turns, the tree-lined road gives way to a more open landscape. We pass the Grand Case Airport and the area begins to look more western with larger strip malls and accompanying parking lots. One of the major complexes is the Leader Price supermarket. It has a modern aluminum and glass exterior with a substantial red diamond shaped sign across the front of the store.

We travel a bit farther down the road past the neighborhoods of Cul de Sac and Hope Estate when Shanie instructs Joyce to make a right onto Rue De Jardins. This is an exclusive, gated neighborhood consisting of about 40 homes. There are two lanes into the community. One is for entering, the other for exiting. Each has its own gate and to the right of the exit lane are several dumpsters for the community's garbage and recyclables. As we drive in, I notice these overflowing dumpsters, as well as many plastic garbage bags lining the road. It's an odd omen that such a nice neighborhood is overdue for garbage collection.

We drive up the roadway as Shanie is scanning from side to side trying to recollect the exact route to Villa Haiku. After a wrong turn and a deft Y-turn maneuver by Joyce, we arrive at the security gate to Villa Haiku.

"Thank you so much Joyce, what do we owe you?"

"$40 would be fine," she laughs.

I give her $50 and feel like I haven't paid her enough. The security gate to Villa Haiku begins to slide back and I start unloading the many bags of supplies and luggage. A tall, fit man with long curly white hair, a fully unbuttoned short-sleeve shirt, a pair of work gloves, worn leather work boots, and carrying pruning shears walks up the steep driveway. He Could easily pass as the better-looking brother to the Christopher Lloyd's , Emme "Doc" Brown character from the "Back to the Future" movies. He speaks politely to Joyce in French and they both laugh. Joyce then turns to us for hugs and good-byes. We thank her again and again for her amazing help and attitude.

As Joyce drives away I turn to meet Alain Pages and instantly like him. He has a natural demeanor of happiness with an equal dose of casual charm.

"I know, it looks like a lot, but we wanted to come prepared," I off to Alain as he admires the amount of supplies we piled onto his driveway.

"No worries, let me show you where you'll be staying, fol low me," He replies as he heads down the steep driveway. Shanie and I grab a few bags and trail him. This is my first chance to see the entirety of the property and it is overwhelmingly impressive.

The Indonesian-styled villa consists of the large living room pavilion, a cottage where the kitchen and office are located, another cottage for the master bedroom and bath. These three areas are centered around the pool deck complete with a deep, black tile-lined dipping pool. The view of Orient Bay are breath-taking and the tropical plants tastefully placed in and around the buildings further enhance this island paradise. There are dozens of palm trees, low-lying, lush green shrubs and a banana-tree garden behind the lower bungalow. As I walk down the driveway, you get a better feeling for the massive open-air pavilion/outdoor living room. Situated perfectly, framed by the large wooden door frame is a white marble, five foot-tall smiling Buddha statue.

We continue down the driveway to the backside of the property. Constructed directly underneath the pavilion is a concrete-walled apartment. It has two bedrooms with a living room and a kitchen seperating the sleeping areas. There are three sliding glass patio doors. One for each bedroom and a third for the entryway directly into the living room. As we cross the large flat parking area, I see the final building of the Villa Haiku property - the lower bungalow. It also mirros the Indonesian-style construction of the two top level cottages and pavilion; complete with ceder shake roof and beautiful, weathered wood construction.

"Here is the bungalow you and Shanie will be staying in," informs Alain as he leans his pruning shears against a large blue dumpster on the driveway.

The bungalow has two sets of double doors and both are open. One set of doors leads to a small living area and kitchen, the other set is the entrance into a large bedroom with two beds. We drop the first load of supplies in the living room and begin to head back up the driveway to collect our remaining supplies.

There is a landscaping crew on the grounds, trimming the bushes and shrubs as well as thinning the palm fronds from all the palm trees.

"We are thinning all the trees to better protect them from the hurricane winds," Alain says to Shanie and me.

"Ahhh, gotcha."

"We'll grab everything else, while you keep working with the gardeners," suggests Shanie. Alain happily nods in agreement.

As we get to our pile of supplies at the top of the driveway, I pause and look at the incredible view of Orient Bay.

"This place is incredible." I grab my wife to bring her close to me.

"I told you so," Shanie replies with a smile and a tightening embrace.
"We're gonna be okay," she adds.

"Yes, I think so, too."

After storing the last of our supplies in the bungalow, we walk up to the kitchen cottage. Alain's wife, Martine, has just returned from shopping and it's my first chance to meet her. She is a stylish and beautiful brunette. Her bright eyes and inviting smile accompany a no-nonsense demeanor and a quiet, impressive intellect. She purposefully moves throughout the kitchen and I get the immediate sense she knows how to get things done.

In one of her shopping bags, Martine removes two solar-powered lanterns as well as rolls of metal tape.

"These are for the remaining glass panels. Shanie can help me finish those up tomorrow," she adds.

But Alain and I are like two excited kids on Christmas morning with the solar powered lanterns. These are new to both of us and we each grab one to get a closer look. They have the traditional propane lantern design, but the top is a solar panel and, instead of the white nylon sock that glows when lit, it is a fluorescent bulb.

Alain and I hand back the lanterns to Martine and he suggests that perhaps it is time for Rosé. We all agree and glasses are passed around, Alain, Martine, Shanie and I raise them and "Salute" to "new friends" and "whatever comes our way."

He suggests we drive down to the sea for a look and a dip into the waters. The beach was stunningly clean, the water temperature perfect and much to my surprise, parts of the beach are what the locals call "naturalist," which just means swim suits are optional. Both Alain and I opt to keep our suits on and dive into the waters, enjoying the view.

We swim for about 20 minutes and towel off before heading back to the car. We walk the beach back to the parking area, I notice quaint homes on the water's edge. I see several beach bars, specifically the "Waikiki" as well as hundreds of homes neatly packed along the shoreline that comprise Orient Bay. It's a very special place to be. We continue down the beach when Alain and Martine call out to a family of four playing in the water.

The husband, Georgie, is a local musician who they befriended by attending many of his shows. He, his wife, young son and daughter are all "naturalists" simply enjoying the Caribbean Sea. Georgie has a 5-gallon water jug in his hand and fills it up with the sea water and attempts to pour it out over his kids' heads, much to the giggles and shrieks of his son and daughter. It's a family spending time together in the water.

We all know the hurricane is out there heading our way, but for now she is far from this idyllic setting.

A few hundred yards into the bay Alain and I watch a couple sailboats bobbing in the small waves. They are about 40 yards apart and each tethered to a mooring ball. One of the sailors is busy tightening his lines, and checking all the port windows. Alain and I can't believe he would try and weather the hurricane here.

We then make our way up the beach to the parking lot and stop at the local grocery store called "Little Casino." We want to purchase some extra El Presidente Beer. The shop is busy with locals buying waters and food supplies, but it isn't frenetic or chaotic. The residents are buying what they can carry. The area beach bars and shops are all busy prepping for Irma. The wave runners are being loaded onto trailers, and some of the businesses are trying to remove portions of the roofs and shuttering their windows. Alain turns to me and prophetically says, "You know, none of this will be here after the hurricane."

In my mind, I am immediately catapulted back to our original condo in Marigot and the thoughts of being relocated to a first-floor unit. Like most of us who have witnessed Katrina, Harvey and Sandy...storm surge is as lethal as the winds. I felt blessed to be with Alain and Martine on high ground.

We drop the beer in the bed of the truck and continue walking around Orient Beach. Alain wants to stop into a local restaurant called, La Place -Le Village D'Orient. We walk under an archway with a backlit, colored sign, the gradient aqua colors of the sign mirroring the shades of the Caribbean. The arched sign is supported by two colonial posts topped with gorgeous white lamps that illuminate the white posts. It is getting to be dusk and the backlit sign is beautiful against the darkening sky. I notice the upper part of the "L" in La Place is in the shape of a heart. I understand why the locals love this little area. It is peaceful, approachable and so much a part of their island life.

We stroll across a large uncluttered area, around a centered palm tree to three open air and partially roofed restaurants. Each comfortably nestled against each other, one restaurant spilling over to the next. A large family is dining in one of the restaurants. They are seated outside as a waitress brings them drinks. They look relaxed and happy.

Alain and Martine enter the center restaurant looking for the proprietor. Martine tells us that their daughter worked as the "Host" last summer, and they would like to check-in on the owner and say "hi" before the hurricane. He greets them near one of the tables and they all chat for about five minutes. They speak in French, as he thanks Alain and Martine for stopping in. But he needs to get back to his customers. I watch them smile and hug. After the short visit, Alain and Martine walk towards us and we all walk under the lighted arch entryway to the truck.

Our next stop is the Rancho Del Sol restaurant that mimics a Tex Mex establishment found in Scottsdale more than a fine French restaurant on Saint Martin. The exterior sign includes a large horseshoe and two six shooters. Shanie and I feel right at home. The restaurant is located on a nearby hill just outside Alain and Martine's neighborhood of Les Jardins des Orient. Since we are the last customers of the evening, we have our choice of outside tables. We order a bottle of wine and, with drinks in hand, in one direction we view Villa Haiku and in the other direction, the Caribbean Sea. The sun is setting as we place our orders. After dinner, we joke that the waitress better run the credit card bill now, because who knows if there will be power tomorrow after the hurricane.

Before we turn in for the night, Alain suggests we toast with some of his handcrafted rum. We meet up at the pavilion. Alain pours us shots and we celebrate our new friendship and hope the storm spares us. Looking over to the giant marble buddha, we decide it might be a good idea to toast him as well.

Alain pours a shot, walks over to the buddha, rubs his belly and raises the glass to buddha's lips. It's a wonderful gesture and we applaud him.

Shanie and I hug our friends good night and venture to our bungalow. We are safe and content. For now.

WOODEN STORM SHUTTERS

The lower bungalow's room air conditioner and ceiling fans do a great job during the night keeping Shanie and I comfortable against the island's summer heat and humidity. Unfortunately, from the abundance of Rosé, El Presidente beers, glasses of French wine and the late-night rounds of homemade rum during our dinner and late-night socializing with Martine and Alain, I'm hungover.

I normally don't mix different alcohols, sticking to either Malbec or light beers, so my head is not happy and a low-grade migraine is trying to escalate into something more wicked. I press the palm of my hand into my right eye in hopes to release some of the pressure. It sorta works, but I'll need some Excedrin soon to stave off a full-on migraine, so I amble into the bungalow's newly remodeled bathroom. I turn on the expensive-looking faucet and fumble in our dab kit searching for the small bottle of Excedrin Migraine. Relief is on the way.

The next order of the day is to get the automatic drip coffee maker to do its thing. Shanie and I bought a good amount of ground coffee with our supplies from Marigot. The automatic coffee maker is easy to locate, but I cannot find any of the saucer-looking coffee filters. It doesn't take long to scan the small kitchen's cupboards and drawers, but to no avail. I decide to find Martine and ask for assistance. I open the kitchen's double doors to the bungalow and am greeted by a beautiful sunrise and the unforgettable calls of several roosters located somewhere in the neighborhood. Exiting the bungalow, I walk up the stairway to the pool deck, go around the pool and see the door to the kitchen cottage is open and Martine is busy pulling supplies from the refrigerator.

"Bonjour. Do you have any coffee filters for the bungalow coffee maker?" My head feeling the curative powers of the Excedrin on my migraine.

Martine looks through a couple of cupboards and pulls out a box of cone-shaped filters as she asks about how we slept. I let her know everything is perfect. I don't happen to see Alain anywhere, so I head back to the bungalow to fix Shanie her cup of morning joe. I take out one of the cone filters and flatten it a bit, scoop the coffee grounds, fill the reservoir and watch as the coffee machine does its thing.

I hear Shanie call from the bungalow and bring her a mug. For a few quiet moments we sip our coffee. I break the calm.

"It is so nice to be here. I feel safer."

"I'm glad, too. I think it's the right decision," she says as she hands me her coffee mug, which is my signal for a refill.

"Must be good coffee today!" I reply. She nods affirmatively.

I tell her to take her time and I'm going to find Alain and see what he's thinking we should accomplish today.

"I'll be up in a few moments to help Martine," she says, looking around the bedroom for her flip flops.

I meet up with Alain in the pavilion enjoying his coffee and appears to be in no real rush to get the day started. After a few more sips and enjoying the view of the sunrise over Orient Bay, we decide the first thing will be to secure all the furniture located in this outdoor living space. There are two white leather couches, two large coffee tables, a large free-standing bar, several decorative trunks and the impressive, white marbled buddha statue.

As I look around the living room, I notice that Alain and Martine have already been at work and moved some stuff into a large storage compartment in the far, north corner of the pavilion. It's a six-foot by six-foot storage area with a tall ceiling complete with two lockable, pull-down garage style steel doors.

We set down our coffees and begin to load deck chairs, a plant stand, bar stools and other decorative items in the storage shed. We roll two area rugs and store them as well.

The two white couches will be stored in the master bedroom cottage. We start pulling off the large soft pillows to lighten the load before carrying each couch. I grab one end as Alain lifts the other and we carry them across the tiled floor, down four steps from the pavilion to the pool deck, across the deck into the master bedroom. We place the couch alongside the large bay window and decide the second couch can simply rest atop this one.

After getting both couches stowed, we want to relocate one of the large coffee tables. I go to raise one end of this teak table and am dumbfounded by the weight of it.

"Holy shit, this is heavy!"

Alain shrugs and laughs, "I know, I try not to move it much."

Alain always has a smile on his face and never seems to worry. It's an admirable trait that will be tested over the next several days.

We are really not sure what to do with this heavy coffee table, so we decide to just place it against one of the pavilion's two interior walls. We turn our attention to the marbled buddha statue. But since we have no way of relocating it, he will stay put.

We hear Martine in the open-air attic above our heads. The previous owner built a massive attic storage space directly underneath the roof of the pavilion. It has no walls and the floor is suspended by the roof trusses. There is a narrow wooden staircase leading up to the attic with a sharp right turn near the top. It's virtually impossible to store anything of size in this space. The staircase railing is comprised of individual, three-foot pieces that resemble a small sailboat's rudder. Each rail post is freestanding on the staircase. There is no handrail connecting them all. While they are beautifully stained and have smooth, rounded sides and top, it's an odd addition to the otherwise Indonesian design of Villa Haiku.

Martine shouts down from the attic that there are two keepsake trunks that need to be relocated. I go up the steps and at the top of the landing have to duck my head to avoid a massive roof truss. There are only two storage trunks in the attic to move.

"I'll get those for you."

Martin offers to help carry them, but they're not heavy.

I pick up one of the trunks and, as I go down the staircase, hold it about shoulder height so I don't bump it against each railing piece. Both trunks are stored in the master bedroom next to the white couches.

Returning to the pavilion, we clean out the small fridge behind the free-standing bar. The free-standing bar is next to the corner shed.

Alain uncoils a red and white rope that looks like it was once used to divide lanes in a swimming pool and ties the bar, a bookcase and an Asian trunk all together in hopes of protecting them against Hurricane Irma's winds.

Pleased with our progress, we head to the kitchen cottage and the glass-paneled safety railing. These railings safeguard you from falling six feet from the kitchen cottage level down to the pool deck.

For most of the morning, Shanie and Martine have been busy

taping Xs on all the glass panels alongside the pavilion above the apartment.

Two of the panels are loose on their footings and easily rock back and forth. They need to be secured. We kneel down by one of the panel's posts and see a small cover on the base. Alain hands me the correct Allen wrench.

As Alain goes to retrieve a socket set, I walk down the steps to the pool deck and to a handyman storage area located directly underneath the footing of the railing. Extra gallons of paint, spare wood pieces, assorted planters and clay pots, miscellaneous pool supplies, garden hoses and a few bicycles are all stored here.

I enter the shed and look up to the ceiling. I can see the mounting bolts that secure the glass railing post. I step outside and suggest to Alain that he unscrew the mounting bolts and completely remove the railing. Alain gives me a thumbs up and starts to wrench the bolts. Once we have removed the glass panels and posts, they are stowed away.

Shanie and Martine return from taping the remaining glass panels and decide it's time for lunch.

Lunch, and in fact all meals for the Pages, is a vital part of their routine. Martine and Alain are excellent cooks and creative in their combinations of meal planning. For today's lunch, they serve vegetables, pasta, sausage and bread. All meals also include a glass of chilled Rosé and cheese for dessert.

At lunch, we discuss, with the projected strength of Irma, that Shanie and I should move in with Martine and Alain in the concrete apartment beneath the pavilion. The apartment has lockable, accordian-style metal hurricane shutters, offering better protection from strong winds and flying debris. Since Shanie and I won't be in the bungalow, we can now use that space to stow away additional furniture and miscellaneous items.

Conversations are easy between us and everyone feels the bonds of friendship strengthening.

After lunch and clearing the table, we are re-energized and eager to accomplish as much as possible in the next 10 hours before Irma makes landfall.

As Alain and I move the large orange leather couch from the porch of the apartment, we discuss where he should park his Ford WildTrak 4x4 pick-up truck.

I suggest he should back it up against one of the double doors of the bungalow.

"Also, for whatever reason, during the hurricane, if we have to leave in a hurry, the truck is pointed in the right direction to flee up the driveway."

Alain agrees. Before he backs up the truck to the bungalow's bedroom double doors, I need to lock and secure the outer wooden hurricane doors and then the interior glass doors.

Afterward, I grab our suitcases and wheel them from the bedroom, through the kitchen, and out of the bungalow's other set of double doors. For these doors, the deadbolt system is on the exterior of the door. After sliding the wooden deadbolt, the doors are still loose on their hinges. Because the wooden hurricane doors are larger than the door frames, we opt to drill wood screws directly through the door into the bungalow's wood siding. Unfortunately, Alain does not have many of these screws, so regrettably only a few are used to secure the door against the siding.

Our next move is to install the two wooden hurricane shutters protecting the master bedroom's bay window. It's a simple system and, similar to the bungalow's hurricane doors, they are oversized. There is an upper and lower wooden guide rail to slide a wooden shutter in from the right, and another from the left, and then the wooden deadbolt to latch.

Alain needs to make a quick trip to the pharmacy for nicotine patches and asks if we need anything else. Shanie suggests he get some more Imodium. Martine is confused.

"If I get a bug, I'll want to get it out of me as fast as I can," she chimes in causing us to all laugh.

Shanie explains her research on a hurricane emergency kit and Imodium was on the list. Obviously, I'm a huge fan of Imodium from my troubles on the day we departed for Saint Martin.

Before Alain leaves for the pharmacy, he asks if I could secure a pile of wood furring strips leftover from repairs to the master bedroom's roof.

"Where do you think I should put them?"

"How about under the steps from the pavilion to the pool deck," he suggests, lighting up a cigarette and turning towards the car-port and the Pages other car, a Kia Piccanto.

Walking around the master bedroom cottage, I locate the fur-ring strips piled up against the back-exterior wall. They vary in length from ten to twelve feet, a half-inch thick and two-inches wide. I grab a few and carry them to the pool steps.

The architect of Villa Haiku did a great job utilizing space for storage. The four steps leading from the pool deck to the pavil-ion are long and the vacuum of space underneath is perfect for storing all the pool supplies. It is also a perfect spot for stowing the faring strips.

After several trips, I finish up and take a break at a small wooden table outside the kitchen when Alain returns and tosses me the box of Imodium.

He relays the pharmacy was out of nicotine patches, but other-wise everything seemed normal in town. We discuss the remaining projects to shore-up the property. There are shutters needed for the kitchen windows, protection for the oversized sliding glass pavilion doors, and we need to relocate a wrought iron skillet and propane tank to the lower apartment. Alain and I walk around the kitchen cottage to a sitting area with a wooden table where they store the outdoor, wrought iron skillet.

We decide to leave the skillet on the ground and just carry the propane burner and tank to the apartment.

Shanie and Martine are busy wrapping photo albums in polystyrene and organizing the insurance documents, titles, deeds and other important, family records. They make several trips to stow them in one of the apartment's cabinets.

The upstairs pavilion only has two walls, the other two sides are open for unimpeded views of Orient Bay and for easy access to the kitchen, master bedroom cottage and the dipping pool. One wall faces the entrance to the property and the driveway's security gate. Alain suggests we leave these doors open and against the outer wall of the pavilion during the hurricane so the wind can blow through the pavilion; and not get trapped underneath the roof. Hopefully, sparing it from damage.

The heavy sliding glass doors don't have hurricane shutters and could easily be shattered by flying debris, so we need to somehow protect them. Plus, we can't lift them off their rails to store them somewhere else. They are simply too large. Alain suggests we use two spare plywood sections stored below the pool deck. He is unsure of their original use, but thinks we could sandwich the glass doors between the pavilion wall and the plywood. We secure the plywood planks and decide we are done for the day.

I haven't seen Shanie much today and go looking for her. I miss her. I find her helping Martine with dinner. The rice is finished and she is sautéing sausage and vegetables. I come up behind her for a hug and hold her for a moment.

"Okay, that's enough," she playfully pushes me away. "I'm working here."

As she chops vegetables, Alain enters the apartment. He opens a bottle of Rosé and we toast to the success of our day. The conversation flow is easy with laughs and many toasts for the good job we all did today to protect Villa Haiku from Hurricane Irma.

After dinner, I decide to take a nap so I'm rested and alert when Irma comes ashore sometime after midnight. None of us have any idea what is truly barreling our way.

HURRICANE IRMA

Alain and I are alone on the front patio, listening to the sounds of the approaching storm. It is close now. We can feel it. The mélange of ocean waves crashing, the wind churning and churning in a counter-clockwise motion, the trees noisily bending and swaying trying to resist the wind that is constantly increasing in velocity.

We look at each other.

It's time.

He picks up his guitar as we make our way into the apartment.

To lock the hurricane shutters, we first close those protecting Alain and Martine's side of the apartment. For the shutters protecting the living room patio doors, I have to press them together from the outside as Alain engages the lock from the inside. I hold them together until I hear a click signifying the lock is secure. Alain pulls on the doors to confirm the lock is holding. Not wanting to spend any more time outside, I quickly proceed to the sliding patio door for our bedroom and fortunately, I can lock these shutters from the inside.

Alain and Martine retreat to their side of the apartment as Shanie and I head into our bedroom. From our respective rooms, we all listen as the storm winds begin to build around us. Within minutes, the gusts become violent and shake the entire apartment.

"Crack." "Crack." "Crack." "CRACK!"

I hear gunfire. Powerful short shots, possibly from a high-powered rifle. The rifle shots occur all around us. We can't make sense of why someone would be firing a rifle during the storm. The wind speed just keeps building and building and seems to be slamming into the apartment from all sides.

"Crack." "Crack." "Crack." "CRACK!"

After several more rifle shots, I sense the need to check on Alain and Martine. As I open our bedroom door to the living room, the noise level becomes instantly more apocalyptic. In desperation, Alain and Martine are frantically moving about with towels and buckets. Their room is on the north side of the apartment and is taking the full force of Hurricane Irma's north wind. Water is flowing around their bedroom's window frame and the patio door's hurricane shutter is violently slamming into the glass of the door. We yell at each other to be heard.

"What the fuck is happening?" I shout. Surprised at how different the hurricane is affecting their side of the apartment.

"Help me roll up some towels, we need to slow the water coming in!"

"Absolutely. Do you know what is causing those rifle cracks?" I scream.

"I think those are trees snapping."

"CRACK!"

"This is fucking insane!" I holler back.

We place towels around the inside window ledge as the glass panes and shutters continuously and ferociously shake. The sound is deafening. Looking closely at the window, the hurricane winds are forcing water underneath and around the glass seals as well as around the window frame itself. Our only option is to try and slow the water streaming in with towels and pray the window frame doesn't explode into the bedroom.

Martine is mopping the walls to keep the water from pooling onto the floor, as we deal with the bedroom window. The hurricane shutters protecting their patio suffer the violent, and now constant, 185 m.p.h. winds. The evil cacophony of vicious shaking makes us all feel, for the first time, that our lives are in real danger.

All of the sudden my ears feel a sinking pressure drop. I'm deaf. As I pinch my nose to balance the pressure to get my hearing back, the glass patio panels curve outwards and then bend back inwards. It's as if they have morphed into the consistency and shape of contact lenses. The ear pressure change is a precursor to the savage wind gusts that reach over 225 m.p.h. Every time we feel the pressure drop in our ears, category 5 wind gusts slam into Villa Haiku. We experience these sickening pressure drops continually for the next six hours.

Outside trees continue to snap accompanied by unknown creaks and slams from objects above our heads. It's an orchestra of destruction. We have no idea what is being demolished above our heads, outside our doors, or elsewhere on the island.

Alain grabs his mother's antique barometer mounted in a wooden shadow box. The gold needle is bouncing up and down. Normally, a barometric needle's movement is not perceptible. This needle is like a nervous two-year old desperate to pee. We are shocked as we watch the needle bouncingly descend. It is on a determined downward progression.

On a normal, sunny day, the barometric reading will be around 30 millibars. For Hurricane Irma, we watch it hurriedly fall below 915 millibars; one of the lowest recorded readings in history. Alain places the treasured heirloom against a wall in our bedroom.

As we struggle to stem the rain pouring in and around the bedroom window, all around us we hear the sickening rifle cracks as more and more palm trees are snapped in half. Suddenly there is a loud sliding sound and violent crash above our heads. The concrete apartment is being assailed by mother nature, and catastrophic wind gusts are shaking the entire structure as if in a major earthquake. The frequent and sudden air pressure drops cause us to constantly stop what we are doing to try and equalize the pressure in our ears. I have to plug my nose, close my mouth and try and exhale into my mouth to release the pressure. I feel the need to check on Shanie in our bedroom. I find her sitting up in bed and frantically working her iPad. She is busy trying to find any updates from the NHC and NOAA. Unfortunately, the next update is scheduled for 5:00 a.m., so we are clueless as to where we are in terms of Hurricane Irma's path.

I check my watch. It is 3:30 a.m. and Irma has been over us for just about an hour and a half. I look to Shanie when suddenly the decibel level of the wind noise substantially increases. It sounds like we are surrounded by hundreds of jet engines on full power, all just feet away from us. Alain and Martine hurriedly enter our room and slam the door behind them. They immediately push one of the twin beds up against the door.

"One of our patio doors just exploded." Alain shouts to us. "There is glass everywhere."

We all stare at each other as the savage winds scream outside. The noise is so equally deafening and horrifying that we become paralyzed with fear and helplessness. There is no way to shout or communicate above the destructive sounds all around us. As something large and heavy slides across the tiled floor above our heads and crashes into something unknown, we simultaneously realize we are now completely at the mercy of whatever guiding fates control our futures. I look to Shanie who looks to me as I turn to Martine who then shifts her focus to Alain. Nothing more can be done.

For the next hour I sit against the wall that separates the bedroom from the bathroom. Shanie, who decides to put in earplugs, sits against another bedroom wall, and Martine and Alain sit atop a twin bed. We are all lost in our shared, but private, hell.

Observing Shanie sitting on the floor, I flashback to when I found her sitting against a bathroom wall a few days after her cancer surgery. She was alone. In the dark. Sobbing. The trauma of her bilateral mastectomy catching up to her. The physical and emotional pain and the confrontation with mortality all ripping away her core. The only way Shanie could battle against all of this was to wail away in the blackness of the room. I lightly rapped on our bathroom door, entered and sat beside her for the next hour or so, holding her, saying nothing. Her sobs finally giving way to slow and steady breathing.

This is how she looks now as the runaway locomotive train that is Irma continues thrashing everything outside. There is no letup as trees snap in half, unknown flying objects slam heavy against our exterior concrete walls, and the relentless winds hauntingly scream as they violently try to penetrate the steel hurricane shutters.

But, we are silent as the world comes noisily apart around us. Shanie does not cry or scream out. She has faced mortality before and was victorious. She is not afraid. I'm terrified.

Around 4:30 a.m. I notice a sliver of light from underneath the hurricane shutter. The impact of this hopeful ray immediately brings us out of our quiet, solitary minds. Frightful darkness of night is giving way to the relief of daybreak. We are a group again.

Alain reaches for the barometer and whether it was pure hope, wishful thinking or an actual progression of the storm, the needle makes a subtle, almost imperceptible tick upwards.

"Did you see that?" Alain shouts to us all.

None of us responds. He shouts it again, as loud as he can. "Did you see that? The barometer might be rising!"

With the growing light level in the bedroom, we can now look at each other and we are all confused and not understanding what Alain is trying to communicate. He doesn't give up and shouts again pointing to the barometer needle, "Did you see that?" It moved.

I look to him. I see his mouth moving, but hear no words over the roar of the wind.

Frustrated that no one can hear him, he emphatically points to the barometer and then motions his hand with forefinger pointed upwards. He looks to each one of us and repeats the motion with his hand.

The gesture sends chills throughout my body. I now know that the needle moving back up means that at least part of the storm is traveling past us. After hours of the needle bouncing in its downward motion, this slight movement up is change. It is hope.

We have no power, no cell phone connections, no way of knowing how anyone else is faring during this storm. But, we now have daylight and the barometer, however subtle, has ascended.

As if the barometer controls the hurricane, we begin to feel and hear the mayhem that is this train slowing down as if it's pulling into a station for a reprieve.

"We must be getting near the eye of the storm!" shouts Alain. As he finishes the word "storm," we now all can clearly hear him. This abrupt, now-clear voice causes us all to laugh aloud and the energy in our bedroom drastically changes to the positive. We are shocked we can actually hear each other. This revelation causes us to stand up and start moving about the room, we are eager to do something other than sit and think.

The winds have drastically subsided. After hours of seemingly endless destruction, silence begins to return to our world.

The barometer is now clearly making a move upwards. It's a smooth and steady climb.

"We are in the eye of the storm," Alain confirms to us.

I quickly cross the room and reach for the bedroom door and turn the handle. I feel no pressure or resistance. I turn to Alain, "I think it's okay to open the door."

Alain nods and we each grab one end of the mattress that we stretched across the door and lift it back onto the box spring. I cautiously crack the door open and peer into the living room through the small crevasse between the door frame and the door. To my utter surprise the room is completely lit up as if all the lights have been turned on. I'm confused as to why it is so bright, when I know we have lost all power.

For a moment, I'm lost, until I mentally connect the dots and recall that the bedroom glass patio door exploded during the night. It is morning light that is pouring into the bedroom and living room, exposing a haphazard mess of leaves, water, debris and glass. Surprisingly, the destruction is mostly contained to the bedroom. The wall that divides bedroom and living room has remarkably protected the living room from the brunt of the first part of Irma.

All four of us walk through the living room into Martine and Alain's bedroom. There is no door to the bedroom. It is just a large, opening cut from the wall that divides the living room and the master bedroom.

There are leaves and other green-type plants plastered every-where. They are stuck to walls, windows and the ceiling. It's like someone has used a leaf blower to spray the entire bedroom with debris. The king-size bed is littered with large branches, dirt and glass shards. Equally surprising to the living room being spared, are the bed sheets, while covered in debris, are still tucked into the mattress. It's like they had been chained down over the mattress. Mother Nature is ruthless, but at the same time, she will spare things seemingly in random grace.

I walk through the bedroom to a small entry room where the sliding patio doors are located. This is a six- by six-foot area with floor-to-ceiling shelves along the long bedroom wall. This is location where one of the sliding patio doors had shattered. The other sliding door remains intact, protected by the remaining half of the steel sliding hurricane shutter. The other shutter was ripped away and has landed, mostly intact, some feet away at the base of a palm tree.

I step over a large brown table that is now upside down with all four legs snapped off. It somehow ended here in front of the broken sliding door. I cautiously peer outside.

"Be careful," Shanie reminds. "We don't know how long the eye will last."

"I will. Let's just see what we can see," I assure her.

To my surprise, looking outside it doesn't look as bad as I was expecting. It's cloudy and misty so I can only see about 20 yards in either direction. There is a gentle, but steady breeze and a whitish foggy opacity everywhere I look. I scan across the lower parking area and to the bungalow to the right. One of the palm trees has fallen across its roof line and the two doors to the living room area have been blown away. Alain's pickup truck that we placed in front of the other bungalow doors looks intact. The windshield may have cracked, but it's hard to tell from our vantage point.

I can't remember how the bungalow roof looked prior to the storm, but to me it appears okay. Something later in the morning we discover to be completely untrue.

The calmness of the hurricane eye lets us do a quick clean-up of Alain and Martine's' bedroom. There is glass everywhere from the shattered patio door, as well as branches, leaves and other blown-about household items. We clean the glass and leaves from their king-size bed and decide the best thing would be to wrap the entire bed in a large blue tarp. This will help protect it from the additional rain and wind expected with the return of the back half of the storm.

By the time we finish with the bed, we can feel the wind increasing and decide to quickly head back to the protection of the bedroom. Alain is certain that the back half of the hurricane will not be as severe for our location at Villa Haiku. The winds will rotate 180 degrees and will now blast the property from a southerly direction. The kitchen and master bedroom cottages both have part of a rocky ridgeline that protects them, and our apartment will be mostly shielded by the lower bungalow.

It's surprising how the daylight has positively affected our moods. We all feel relatively good considering what we endured, and are eager to talk about how we think we have weathered the worst of Irma. Alain's barometer confirms our growing confidence that we are going to survive.

The second half of the storm seems to move quicker. We don't feel the massive pressure drops, nor does the barometer needle move as rapidly and as far downward as it did during the night. We no longer hear the battering of violent noises like we did during the night.

Around 10:00 a.m., we believe that Hurricane Irma has moved farther west of Saint Martin and we open the bedroom door to assess our world at Villa Haiku. There is no power and no cell phone connection, so we are all alone on our interpretation of the storm's progress.

We leave our bedroom and decide to exit the apartment through the broken patio door of Alain and Martine's bedroom. I stick out my head and surprisingly notice no real change from the eye of the storm. The patio door is elevated about two feet off the ground and, for some reason, there are no steps to help descend to the driveway level. The safest way is to sit down on the stoop and then lower my legs to the ground. Martine, Alain, Shanie and I carefully navigate the big drop and then continue to walk across the lower parking level to get a better vantage point to look back at the pavilion above our heads and the rest of the Villa Haiku buildings.

In almost a slo-motion, surreal gesticulation, Martine's knees buckle and her hands slowly go to cover her face. A muffled wail escapes between her cupped hands.

"Oh Alain. Oh Alain!!" she cries out as she collapses into his arms.

I cannot see what has caused Martine's reaction until I meet up with her at the far end of the lower parking area and look back at what used to be Villa Haiku.

None of us are mentally prepared to view the near total devastation to all four of the Villa Haiku buildings. The massive roof above the apartment, which was supported by four large diameter Indonesian wood timbers, is mostly blown away. The four massive timbers supporting the roof have lifted off their cement and rebar bases and now the entire roof is listing precariously towards the kitchen building. As we all look up at the pavilion's roof, Alain notices that one immense roof truss is now resting atop the head of the buddha statue.

"Do you see that? The roof is being supported by Buddha!"

We are dumbfounded, looking up at this enormous roof structure being held aloft by the buddha statue. Incredibly, this is the statue we couldn't move during our hurricane prep and it has now prevented the entire roof from crashing down on us during the storm. Who knows what would have happened if the roof had collapsed on us directly below in the lower apartment.

We are momentarily distracted by the miracle of the buddha statue, but then turn our attention back to the destruction of Villa Haiku. Every single safety glass panel in the railings that lined the various ledges and stoops has been torn away and is now strewn all over the property. Only the frames remain, and the some of those are a twisted mess. Most of the glass panels now resemble glass-laden throw rugs. The glass itself shattered into a thousand fragments, held together by a thick, super-adhesive film.

The entire pool deck railing has been destroyed, but most of the steps up the pool deck are intact. The stairwell is protected on three sides by the bungalow, a breezeway, and storage area, and for some reason has become a collection point for all sorts of debris from the hurricane. There are palm tree trunks, several pieces of long grooved ceiling boards, splintered building lumber, leaves and other building supplies. All this debris has been saturated by the torrential hurricane rains.

The master bedroom roof has gaping holes, and the large six-by-six picture window overlooking the pool deck, where we had mounted the wooden shutters, has completely blown into the bedroom. The shutters are nowhere to be seen, and now there is a giant hole where the window used to be.

The lower bungalow roof looks to have suffered major damage from both the high winds and from toppled palm trees. Two of the entry doors have blown away. The other set of bungalow doors protected by Alain's truck seem to have been spared.

Martine continues to quietly cry. We all are emotionally impacted by the level of destruction. No words can ease the shock and disbelief. Alain puts his arm around Martine and hugs her tightly. I reach for Shanie. For several moments, we are all silent.

Alain breaks the silence, in his most charming and comforting manner says, "We'll rebuild!"

His simple, powerful words are the catalyst we all need to begin the immediate pressing concerns of what to do right this minute, post-Irma.

"We need to find the insurance papers, and let's make videos of all the damage," Martine responds to Alain as she regains her composure. She then marches straight back into the apartment to retrieve her cellphone.

For the next several hours, we take videos and pictures of all the damage at Villa Haiku. We are extremely careful as we make our way through the different structures because of all the glass, nails, broken wood planks and beams, branches and the other building materials strewn over the entire property.

Next, we organize our stockpiles. Between what Martine and Alain had stocked up, plus the good amount of supplies Shanie and I had brought with us, we feel we should be able to sustain ourselves for a while. Because there is no power and the toilets need electricity to flush, we decide we should dig a hole for a bathroom. The agreement is to dig it just behind the lower bungalow at a fairly flat area. Although it is not the most private of places to do your business, the fear of cholera supersedes personal privacy.

It is nearing dusk, so Alain and Martine want to prepare dinner. Villa Haiku is the center of our universe. Our isolation, while scary, is also a protective bubble. We have no idea what's happening all over the rest of the island.

And as we discover during the next night as armed marauders try to enter our neighborhood, the island's governments do not have a handle on the severity of the disaster or the plight of its citizenry. Surviving Hurricane Irma is one thing. Surviving the aftermath will be another.

GUNFIRE

The island has no power and no communications. It feels as if we are on our own, fending for ourselves. Alain and Martine's home is destroyed as well as their bread-and-breakfast business, and yet, they insist the four of us make a proper dinner and all sit down together to count our blessings.

Unlike America, where so many of our meals seem to be on the go, our hosts insist we sit down to break bread, converse and be together. At first, I'm shocked by this persistence. There is destruction all around us and we have so much work to do to shore up the property and make it as safe as possible, that I feel we should always be working...to keep going...to not stop and just eat as we work. But, for our first dinner after the passing of Hurricane Irma, amid the complete wreckage of Villa Haiku, we will dine on pasta, vegetables, cheese and dried sausage. Glasses of Rosé are raised and we toast to our survival.

Throughout dinner, we talk about what it would have been like if Shanie and I hadn't made it to Villa Haiku. We would have been very alone in Marigot and we will never know what level of damage our condo or surrounding area would have suffered. Alain and Martine both talk about how hard it would have been to try and secure their large property and most likely, would have left a majority of Villa Haiku unprotected. The four us together suffering through the night, as horrible as it was, was far, far better than riding out the storm just as a couple. We are all exhausted physically and mentally from the violence of the hurricane hitting during the night, as well as the sheer scale of the damage to the property and the day's efforts to begin picking up the pieces, so we all turn in after dinner. Shanie and I fall asleep in each other's arms. We stay that way, wrapped together throughout the quiet and uneventful night.

The morning finds us sitting around the table as Alain prepares coffee using the burner propane stove. I can't imagine what we would have done, if not for Alain's propane stove. As if confirming my line of thinking, Alain hands me a hot, delicious cup. The aroma and taste have an empowering effect.

"We can do this. We can get through this," I think to myself as I sip my coffee, and look out over the porch and all the upheaval around us. My misperception towards the importance of these civilized meals gives way to a greater understanding. It's now easy for me to see how comforting these meals are to each one of us. It's a moment of normalcy in times that are far from normal.

We discuss several tasks that we should accomplish throughout the day. Alain and Martine are rightly concerned about what or what not their insurance will cover and want to review their policy. A next-door neighbor is their insurance agent and they hope he will stop by today.

I will spend most of the day trying to board up window frames as well as start to clear paths and concentrate the debris that has been scattered everywhere.

Before we start, we talk about how everyone needs to be very careful when walking around the damaged buildings. The number of nails from all the torn off roofs, ceiling tiles, shingles, railings, and deck boards is absolutely staggering. We want to make sure everyone is wearing proper footwear when working around the property. Also, we hand out work gloves.

Shanie will work in the cottage housing the kitchen, and will try to sort through the family albums and keepsakes. There is extensive water damage and luckily most of these items had been wrapped in plastic. But, everything of value needs to be re-located to the lower apartment.

Both Martine and Shanie had purchased several bottles of anti-septic spray and want to ensure if we get a cut or scrape to blast it right away with spray. The fear of getting an infection from stepping on a nail or piece of glass is very real and could have serious consequences. We have no idea of the structural integrity of each of the cottages, but it is important to try and help salvage as much of Martine and Alain's personal property, so we implement a buddy system when working in the damaged cottages.

For most of the day, I work in the lower bungalow. The two entrance doors to the living room have blown away, a large window has shattered inwards and it is flooded throughout. Un-fortunately, we stored much of Alain and Martine's expensive furniture in the bungalow's main living area. Very similar to the master bedroom cottage, the bungalow looks as if a tor-nado was set loose inside to purposely destroy as much as pos-sible. Glass, vegetation, drywall, dirt and other debris cake the walls, and the furniture has been spun into a tangled heap. It constantly amazes me how much of the tropical rainforest has ended up inside these buildings. From large leaves to morsels of greenery, it all has been blasted into every tuck and corner of each room.

Before I can start untangling the furniture, I try and sweep out much of the standing water and pick up the shards of glass. For the glass pieces, we try to safely collect and dispose of them in large garbage bags or left-over pool salt bags. For the rest of the debris, the only real option is to add it to the scrap heap the storm caused to collect at the bottom of the pool deck stair-case. It is wet, slimy and hazardous work. I bring out several of the chairs and an Asian-themed curio cabinet that looks in fairly good shape. The expensive, orange Italian leather couch is soaked in rain and salt water, as well as embedded with glass, and is a total loss. Unfortunately, nothing else looks savable.

The next priority for the bungalow is to somehow jerry rig some doors and cover the gaping hole where the living room window used to be.

I walk around to a pile of debris at the bottom of the pool deck stairwell and come across a piece of the bungalow's original door. I pull it out from underneath several pieces of clap board and sections of pool deck railing. Also, scattered atop the many sections of the pool railing are long rafter beams from the bungalow's roof. What is so shocking is that these beams, which are six-inches thick and at least eight-feet in length have been sheared in half along the total length of the beam. I can't even begin to understand the force or physics required to rip a beam in this way.

I bring over the partial door and try and line it up against one of the door jams. Luckily, two of the hinges are attached and useable. But I don't have any screws to mount the hinges to the jam. For the next hour, I go on a scavenger hunt to find nails and screws from all the scrap wood and broken lumber that used to be part of the cottages and bungalows of Villa Haiku. To my utter disbelief, I cannot seem find a straight screw or nail anywhere. Thousands of nails and screws litter the property and all of them are bent at odd angles. I amass a small handful of semi-straight screws and secure the doors.

We are lucky that Alain and Martine had a quality refrigerator inside the apartment. The power has been off for more than 30 hours and yet, all the food inside the refrigerator is cool and unspoiled. We have placed a few of the frozen water bottles inside the refrigerator and they seem to be helping.

For dinner, Alain works the propane burner heating up some vegetables as Martine cuts up some dried sausage and cheese. Shanie and I arrange the table and chairs and set the table. All in all, we are in good spirits. Some of their expensive furniture seems to be salvageable and Martine and Shanie are able to secure many of family photo albums and keepsakes from the kitchen cottage. We quickly finish off a bottle of Rosé and decide to open the box of Cote du Rhone wine for a dessert with some chocolate.

After dinner, I venture out to the end of the parking lot in front of the lower bungalow. I'm standing on a short curb and have a great vantage point of the community entrance. Peppering the sheer darkness are the lights of homeowners who have gas generators and are using them to light up their garages and outdoor home lighting. From this elevated view, I can see the main roadway, the N7, when a couple of vehicles pull into the entrance.

In the front is a pickup truck, and because it is so dark, I can't make out the second vehicle. Suddenly, loud angry shouts fill the night. The neighbors standing guard at the entrance are being harassed by whomever has driven into the community. The shouting continues, and while I can't understand the screams, because it is all in French, it's obvious this is a serious situation. Without any warning I hear a gun shot, quickly followed by another.

The gunfire is terrifying. I run back to the porch for cover. From the safety of the patio, we watch as neighbor after neighbor rush out of their homes, and run to their cars to honk their horns. Others have jumped into their vehicles and are speeding towards the entrance.

Martine instructs us to grab our solar lamps and flashlights. We run to the end of the driveway and aim them down towards the entrance.

This is all part of the neighborhood warning system. The concept is to make the neighborhood appear highly occupied and willing to defend its property and belongings.

It looks like whoever is trying to force their way into the neighborhood is rethinking their plan. The two cars screech their tires as they back up and flee south down the N7 towards Quarter D'Orleans. The quiet night returns to Les Jardens des Orient.

In my life, I've never been around violence involving guns. This shakes me to my core. I'm on an island, thousands of miles from home, suffering through the biggest hurricane on record, and now have to worry about protecting my wife, friends and myself from gun violence.

The severity of our situation raises another level, so we decide it is best to put anything of value inside the apartment and lock ourselves in for the night. After putting the table, propane tank, water bottles, buckets, chairs and anything else that makes it look like we have provisions, we all head inside and try to lock the hurricane shutters.

Alain and Martine's hurricane shutter, although not reattached, loosely hangs on its track, but from the outside looks secure. With all the patio doors shut, and all the hurricane shutters closed, our thinking is that Villa Haiku looks completely abandoned from the road and the level of visible destruction would deter marauders. If someone did try and walk the property at night, they would undoubtedly stumble over the debris causing enough noise to alarm us.

Inside the apartment, the air is stagnant and at least 90 degrees. It's going to be a long, hot night and there is nothing we can do about it. We need to keep everything locked up after hearing those gunshots. Shanie is already on the bed and under the mosquito net. I'm still in my clothes and wearing my shoes; a precaution in case we have to deal with anything during the night. I reach out from under the mosquito net to make sure the can of wasp spray is next to my bed. I check my pocket for my Leatherman. As I lie there in absolute, black darkness, drenched in sweat, I think about the phrase "night terrors" and realize this is probably happening on many parts of Saint Martin this evening.

THE SECURITY GATE

B efore last night's gunfire, I felt I could handle most of the events surrounding the hurricane, but I'm ill-prepared for armed gangs wandering the streets looking to steal anything they can. And with rumors of rapes and murders, it's imperative that we secure ourselves as best as we can, including, finding a way to close the steel security gate to the property.

While preparing Villa Haiku for the hurricane, Alain was advised to leave the security gate open. This allowed the 15-foot portion of the steel gate to safely rest against a concrete property wall, offering a protective backstop of sorts. If the gate were to have been closed and locked during the cyclone, it would have become a giant sail, ripped off its tracks to become a lethal missile in the 225 miles per hour wind gusts.

The gate is made up of three sections. One is the actual 15-foot sliding gate. The second, mounted to the concrete wall is a shorter 4-foot section with an access door. The design of the gate also includes a thicker post section, like a sentry post. This section separates the door from the sliding gate, is two feet taller than the gate, and is topped with a security light.

During the hurricane, a massive palm tree had fallen across the gate, across the access door and is now wedged around the sentry post. The trunk of the tree rests inside the gate while the top of the tree hangs over the roadway. There is no way to slide the gate open. Additionally, another palm tree has been jammed inside the hanging palm tree and completely impedes the sliding security gate. And finally, to make matters even more difficult, both of these trees have been pinned together by yet another tree with a thick trunk. There is no easy way to remove any of one these trees. The only option is to cut them into smaller sections.

With no power on the island, we'll need to use a hand saw. Alain's tool supply includes a pruning shears, a cheaply made tree saw, an expanding ladder, some rope and his Ford Wildtrak truck. It's 9 am and 95 degrees with 100% humidity. Alain and I are drenched just walking up the driveway.

The first thing is to remove all the palm fronds from the tree hanging over the gate and sentry post. This will take weight off the crown and hopefully make the tree easier to pull off the gate. Alain climbs up the ladder and begins to saw. Palm trees have a very unique fibrous or cordage-like network that runs from the trunk to the heart of the tree from where the palms grow. This cordage is soft, heavy and moist. So sawing while not impossible, is slow going and tedious.

In 30 minutes of sawing we have barely make any progress. As we saw deeper into the trunk, the weight of the tree pinches the saw. The blade is constantly bending and flexing, and we are deathly afraid it will snap. We have to constantly widen our cut to help relieve the pressure on the blade.

After another 30 minutes of sawing, it appears we have made a deep enough cut to pull the top off the tree. From the street side, I start to pull the tree away from the post. There is a crack but no movement. Pulling harder does nothing. I try another heave, but the rope slides through my hands and I fall onto the roadway.

Sitting on my ass, I take a breather and scan the landscape. On both sides of the road, lie heaps of trees, branches, tin roof sections, fencing, glass, nails, roof trusses, and fractured lumber of all types and sizes. What once was a lush tropical rainforest is now a barren landscape. A nuclear wasteland.

I'm nearsighted and throughout the hurricane and aftermath, I've switched to wearing my glasses over contact lenses. With no running water and other sanitation issues, sticking muddied fingers in my eyes for a contact lens seems like an unnecessary risk.

I have a habit of hanging my glasses on my tank top. Using one of the arms to hang it on my shirt. After I fall, I instinctively reach to check for my glasses, but they aren't there. And, I can't remember the last time I felt them. I look around, but only find nails, glass and debris. Alain and I widen our search area and uncover what looks like a stripper pole. We look at each other and burst out laughing. "Really? A stripper pole? Maybe I should bring it down for our wives for some evening entertainment."

At this point, all humor is good humor. After some back and forth, we opt to leave the pole where it is, but make sure to let our wives know where it is. Just in case.

We work our way down the steep driveway and Alain calls out. "Billy, I found them!" As he picks up a mangled pair of glasses with one of the lenses missing. I look around and find the other lens. Other than some minor scratches, its fine and I bend the frames back, pop the lens back in and the glasses have some resemblance of the original shape.

Alain and I return to sawing the palm tree and make progress. I walk back outside the gate to the roadway and pull hard on the rope. The top section of the tree begins to give and after more cracking sounds, falls to the ground. We take a moment to drink some water and catch our breath.

"Small victories," I exhale between sips of water.

While the palm tree is no longer wedged around the sentry post, it is still jammed into place by the other two trees. We cut the trunk of the yellowish colored tree and find it to be soft and porous. Sawing takes little effort and in no time have sawed through it.

Alain walks down the driveway to get his pickup truck as I wrap the rope around the topless palm tree still leaning over the gate. I secure the rope to a front hitch on his truck. Alain pops it into neutral and lets the steepness of the driveway coast the truck away from the tree. The rope tightens and the tree begins to move, but then abruptly stops. Alain continues to drift down the driveway, but the stubborn tree isn't budging and within seconds the rope snaps in two.

The yellowish tree trunk is still pinning the large palm tree against the gate, so we need to cut more of the trunk. After a few moments of sawing, we are ready to try again. Alain jumps into the pickup, pops it into neutral and again begins to drift down the driveway. The rope tightens, but holds. The now 15-foot palm tree, with its top sawed off, begins to move and finally, falls off the gate onto the ground. We are overjoyed.

The entire driveway is bordered with a two-foot high concrete edge. We need to drag the fallen palm away from the gate and leave it resting against the concrete edge.
We are successful and high-five each other.

"Small victory," I say.

We use our leather gloves and sticks to clear the gate track of nails and debris. After a short time, Alain looks at me as I stand, ready to try and slide the gate. This is the moment. Is the steel gate severely bent? Will it slide? We each take a deep breath and try and slide the gate. It moves for about 3 inches and then jams.

We try again, but it keeps abruptly stopping. We look closely and recognize that it has lifted off the track and part of it is pinching against a concrete imperfection on the driveway. I walk to the far end of the gate as Alain goes to the other end and we gently lift the entire gate. With the two of us, it is easy to lift, and we reposition it onto the track. We pull on the gate. It slides.

Alain and I can't believe that, after hours and hours of tenuous work, the security gate is operational.

Small victories.

During the time Alain and I were dealing with the gate, Shanie and Martine were busy bringing clothes and salvageable items from the kitchen and master bedroom to the lower apartment. Before Alain and Martin bought Villa Haiku, they were corporate executives for Air France. It was important for Martine to try and save the expensive gowns and business suits they had collected over the years. They strung up several laundry lines in front of the apartment patio and have been hanging as many of them as possible.

As the clothes sway in the tropical breeze, I'm very happy to see my wife. Even though we were on the property all day, we had very little time for any interaction.
I missed her and bring her near to me. We look into each other's eyes.

"Missed you today. But the gate is now closed and locked."

"Nice job. As you can see, Martine and I have been busy as well," she adds before releasing me to plop down into a chair. I sit down next to her and grab her hand in mine. She squeezes it hard, reaffirming. We are content just being close to each other.

Alain suggests a glass of Rosé, and we all immediately say yes. The day has been a success and we are pleased with our efforts.

We toast to each other not knowing that a category 4 hurricane is barreling towards us.

HURRICANE JOSE

The only communication with the outside world is via a small, 9-volt transistor radio. Alain tunes it to a local radio station, Lazer 101. The morning announcer is informing whomever is listening that the island is under an "Orange Vigilance" for Cyclone (Hurricane) Jose and law enforcement is enacting a curfew at dusk.

Vigilance is a comparable to the American weather alert system of "Warning" or "Watch." The severity is determined by the color associated with the vigilance. The colors are yellow, orange, red and purple. Purple being the most dangerous, which is the color associated with Irma.

The announcer keeps repeating information about the curfew and telling listeners to ready property for high winds and torrential rain.

This is the first formal declaration we have heard about police and authorities enacting a curfew. It's been three days since hurricane Irma and only now, under another hurricane threat, do we hear some sort of civil messaging. Prior to this alert, we have heard nothing via public address or official government communiques. Most of the information is from the occasional visit of neighbors, who stop by to check on Alain and Martine, and the two Americans taking refuge at Villa Haiku. The announcer continues that Hurricane Jose could bring torrential rain to the island as it passes over us, so we try and tarp roofs and clear paths for the water to flow over or around your property.

The news about the potential rains is heart wrenching. Villa

Haiku is situated midway up a large ridge with several good-sized estates above us. The 240 miles per hour winds of Irma stripped the mountainside of tropical rainforest vegetation, so to me, we might also be under the threat of landslides.

Adding to this concern is the sheer amount of loose debris that litters the entire property. Shattered glass panels, wood ceiling planks, partial railings, doors, broken tree trunks, shingles and other large roof sections, all these elements and more will become lethal projectiles with expected hurricane winds. There are also gaping holes in many of the roofs and blown-out windows in the other buildings. Any rainstorm will again flood most of the Villa Haiku buildings.

As we finish up our breakfast consisting of last night's noodles, bread, cheese and thankfully, a fair amount of coffee, we discuss the best way to prepare for Hurricane Jose. Alain and I will try to better attach the right half side of the steel hurricane storm shutter for their bedroom. During Irma, this shutter was ripped off its hinges and the glass patio sliding door was shattered. It is imperative to secure this shutter. Otherwise, we have no way to prevent the hurricane winds, rain and debris from flying into the apartment.

Looking closely, we see why the shutter was ripped off its hinges. The shutter is over six feet tall and weighs more than 20 pounds. It was installed with only three undersized concrete anchors.

To properly remount this shutter, we would need a concrete hammer drill, concrete anchors and lots of electricity. None of which we have. We only have a small portable drill with very little battery life, some drywall screws and a few nails that were scavenged from the debris piles. We have no electricity and the portable generator that came with the property when Alain and Martine bought Villa Haiku is buried under a large section of the master bedroom roof. They never got around to testing this old rusted out generator before the hurricane anyway, so it's useless.

Alain inspects the upper and lower tracks for the hurricane shutter and says they are in good shape.

I look at the patio door frame and tap it with a hammer. To my utter surprise. It is made of wood. I'm thinking maybe there is a way to reattach the hurricane shutter with what we have on hand.

We sit on the stoop for a few minutes racking our brains.

After a few moments, I suggest to Alain. "What about using those roof furring strips we stored under the pool steps?"

"Let's cut those to size and hammer one onto the sliding patio door frame. We could repeat this process adding one piece on top of the other until we make up the six inches to the hurricane tract. What do you think?" I visually show him by putting up my hand in a high five, then I place my other hand in front of the high five and repeat this process.

"I think I get what you mean," he confirms. "That could work."

Alain and I cautiously enter the pavilion, walk down the four pool deck steps to the pool level and open the access door below the steps. To our relief, all the furring strips are intact. We pull most of them out until we find the ones that look to be the straightest.

We take them down the lower apartment. Alain measures the height of the door and I go about cutting the strips to 89 inches. While I'm cutting the strips, Alain goes hunting for any extra nails and screws. After about 20 minutes, I have all six pieces ready and we hammer the first piece up against the frame. Once that is secured, we place the next furring strip on top of the one we just placed and hammer them together. We continue this process until we've built out the six inches needed to match up with the hurricane shutter's track.

Alain and I lift the hurricane shutter onto the tracks. Luckily, the hinges for the shutter rotate, so we pivot them until they line up with our furring strip. We take four of the largest screws and spend the next hour screwing the hinges into place. It is agonizing work, but we have no choice. It's got to work.

With the shutter mounted as best as we can. We take a step back and take deep breaths.

"Ready?" I ask him.

"Yeap," He smiles.

I go to the right-side shutter as Alain goes to the left. After some ugly scraping sounds the doors meet on the track and we are able to click and lock them tight.

"Fucking A!" I shout.

"Fucking A is right," Alain replies.

"Unbelievable." Admiring our work.

Alain adds, "small victories."

Our next task is to clear whatever debris piles we can to help rainwater flow around the property. It's also important to clean out many of the drain lids scattered about the property. The drains are part of the rainwater removal pipe system that runs underneath all the buildings of Villa Haiku. The diameter of these white lids is about six inches and I need to find them buried under the piles of vegetation and debris.

As we head up the driveway to the car port, Alain wants to first try and weatherproof Martine's Kia Piccanto. It is parked under the listing carport and is splattered with vegetation. It's almost as if the shreds of leaves and debris are part of the car's permanent paint scheme. The driver's side window is completely gone. I look through the smashed window in awe of the amount of glass that blankets both the front and back seats. Similar to the lower bungalow, it looks like a tornado made its way into the small car, pulverizing the glass into small pieces and embedding them in everything.

Alain heads back down the driveway in search of some tape and a garbage bag.

I step back and look at everything around the car. There are several large tree branches, an insane amount of leaves and uprooted plants as well as a few more sections from the glass railing that was mounted on the other side of the pavilion.

We need to create a channel for the water to flow down the driveway, through the carport to a cement channel that runs alongside the master bedroom building, to the lower bungalow. This cement channel is an integral part of the rainwater removal system for the entire property and it is dammed up with debris. Luckily, most of the debris is small in size and it doesn't us long to clear the channel.

Alain returns with a garbage bag and duct tape. But the tape will not stick to the car's window frame. Alain rubs his hands on the hood of the car and shows me his hand. It is covered in a fine silvery dust.

"Should I have an idea what that is?" I question Alain.

"It is probably salt left behind from Irma's rains." He answers and goes on to explain how hurricane winds create updrafts from the ocean surface, which can cause it to get mixed into the rain clouds.

Taking off my tank top, I use it to wipe down the car's surface. We tape the garbage bag across onto the window and feel we've spent too much time on this project. We need to move on.

I return to finding the drain lids that line the walkway to the pavilion, buried underneath leaves and branches. The next hour is spent clearing off all the steps. It's not hard work, just a matter of shoveling debris to the other side of a retaining wall that lines the steps. I uncover the four drains and clean them off.

Feeling good about the progress I head back to the lower apartment. I'm concerned about one of the air conditioning condenser units. During Irma, this heavy steel unit broke free of its L-brackets and now dangles, suspended only by a thick power cord and two copper tubes. This unit is located just outside the entrance to Shanie's and my side of the apartment. My concern is that in hurricane-force winds, this unit will become a lethal projectile, possibly torpedoing into our bedroom.

I know there is no power on the island, so I take out my Leatherman multitool and use the serrated blade to slice through the power cord. I grab a small crescent wrench and loosen the nut that attaches one of the copper tubes to the top of the unit. It twists easily and immediately I hear a high-pitched screech from invisible gas rapidly escaping the copper tube. The blast hits me, and immediately I feel dizzy and disorientated. I frantically retighten the nut and stagger back to a chair. As I regain composure, I realize one of the tubes was the water line and the other Freon gas. A simple, stupid mistake that could have turned out much worse. I'm tired and need to slow down. We have no way of getting any emergency medical assistance.

The fresh air helps regain my senses and I gingerly walk up the hill to find everyone.

Shanie and Martine have been busy in the master bedroom and thankfully, I feel better by the time I see them coming out of the bedroom door. For some reason, I avoid talking about what happened with the AC unit.

Martine has a beaming smile on her face.

"We found the champagne!" She exclaims. Alain and Martine had recently purchased a case of champagne to store until

Christmas when their three children, spouses and grandkids were all going to vacation in Villa Haiku.

"Since we won't be having Christmas here, we might as well enjoy what we can," Martine exclaims. I follow Martine into the bedroom. The exterior bedroom door is severely bent and will only open part way, so we all have to squeeze through the opening to get into the bedroom. The bedroom looks like someone had tossed a hand grenade into it. Most of the ceiling is gone and the pink and fibrous insulation is flowing down like a waterfall towards the bed. A steady stream of water drips off the insulation onto the ruined bedcoverings and mattress.

Martine nonchalantly points to a box on the floor next to one of the storage trunks from the pavilion's attic. The cardboard champagne case has fragments of glass, part of a soaking shirt or dress and pieces of vegetation all over it.

"Out of the twelve bottles, only six survived," Martine explains as I carefully open the lid a bit farther and shift through the broken, black bottles to find the remaining good ones. I grab four of them.

It takes me several minutes to make the journey out of the bedroom, through the carport, down the steep driveway to the lower level to store the champagne in the apartment kitchen. As I make my way back up the hill, I bump into Alain.

"Say hey! Martine found the case of champagne and six of the bottles survived!"

"Small victories!" He responds with a smile. Alain talks about how he just returned from visiting Jan, the neighborhood president, and that Jan is asking all homeowners to meet early this afternoon down in the grassy area in front of his house for a neighborhood meeting. Jan has been in contact with some of the authorities and a couple of the Gendarmes will be present to give this close-knit community an update.

"You and Shanie can stay here during the meeting, because it will be all in French." And we'll give you any information afterwards. "

"Sounds good to me." I let him know we're working in the master bedroom trying to salvage what we can.

"I've got one more load of paintings to bring to the apartment. Do you have anything you want to do after that?" I ask.

"Oui, when you are finished, let's check the cistern and bring some water down for cleaning dishes and for flushing out the buckets we use as toilets." A cistern is a large inground holding tank for collecting rainwater. Alain and Martine's is located underneath the kitchen cottage.

"Gotcha, give me 15 minutes."

Martine has the two remaining champagne bottles and three of the paintings stacked next to the bedroom door. As, I grab the paintings and champagne bottles, Shanie pops her head out of the door.

"Hey honey, any word about Hurricane Jose?"

"Nothing yet. There is a neighborhood meeting this aft and Martine and Alain are going. Maybe we'll know more then. You good?"

"Yeah, Martine and I are almost done." She smiles and air kisses.

I drop off the paintings and champagne at the apartment where Alain is waiting. We walk back up the driveway to the kitchen. To access the cistern, there is a removable lid on the floor of the attached laundry room. This small room is built off the kitchen cottage and stocked with a variety of laundry soaps, insecticides and other household items. The room was fairly protected from the storm and is in good shape. Alain kneels down and pulls up the heavy lid. He grabs a nearby bucket with about six feet of rope tied to the end of the handle and drops it into the cistern, letting out almost four-feet of the rope until the bucket reaches the water level. He fills up the bucket and hoists it back up through the floor. The water in the bucket looks clear.

"It looks good, but let's drop a chlorine tab into the tank to keep it that way," Alain says as he reaches for a box of tabs.

We fill three large pails of cistern water and carry them down to the apartment.

Martine and Shanie are on the porch trying to tune in the little transistor radio. After several attempts, the station holds and we hear the Lazer 101 announcer relay Jose is progressing in a north by northwest direction and is currently 60 miles north of Saint Martin.

This information quickly gets interpreted differently between Shanie and Martine. Shanie thinks we need to begin to immediately prepare for the hurricane passing by the island.

"It's way too far north," informs Martine. "We aren't in any real danger."

Shanie disagrees, and for several moments they go back and forth about what we should do. It's the first tension we've had since arriving at Villa Haiku.

Alain intercedes and says it's time for him and Martine to attend the neighborhood meeting. While they are away, Shanie and I decide to clean up and store everything we can in case the information is wrong. The weather offers us no clue. The skies are cloud-covered and grey, but no dark horizon. The winds are quiet.

Alain and Martine return from the meeting and inform us of some new developments. It appears there are some armed gangs roaming parts of the island and that is the real reason behind the curfew. Hurricane Jose is well to our north and poses no immediate threat to the island. Authorities were using the hurricane as a justifiable cause to impose the curfew and to try and bring order back to the French side of the island.

The news Hurricane Jose is no threat causes us to burst out in high fives and hugs. We don't even care that a gentle rain is starting to fall. The earlier tension between Shanie and Martine is forgotten. In fact, Alain and Martine suggest taking showers in the rain. It doesn't take us long to strip off all our clothes and dance around in the warm, gentle rain.

I look at my wife, fearless in not only exposing her reconstructed breasts, absent of nipples, but also fearless in embracing our circumstances. I cannot believe the radiance emanating from her.

Martine grabs some bar soap and shampoo and we wash our hair and clean off the sweat and dirt from days and days of hard work. As we celebrate in the nude, one of their neighbors innocently strolls down the driveway to check on us. He gets an eyeful of four naked dancing people, but we don't care. For this brief respite, our spirits are renewed.

ISLAND RUINATION & FACEBOOK PLEAS

The next day's first priority is to pick up Jan, the Les Jardens des Orient neighborhood chairman, and travel into the small hillside community named Concordia. This town is a few blocks from the center of Marigot. Jan is also the principal at the local elementary school, and at last night's neighborhood meeting, informed Alain and Martine that his school had electricity. He offered to let us in to charge our cell phones. We are frantic to communicate with our families and the hope is that with electricity, we might be able to send emails. No one has heard from Shanie and I since the hurricane - four days ago.

Since Irma, I have not traveled beyond the safety and confines of Villa Haiku, so traveling to Concordia will provide me a first-hand view of Irma's impact to much of the French side of the island. Villa Haiku is on the northeast side of the island and will be traveling over the northern route on the N7 and then south into Marigot and Concordia.

As we drive out the entrance to Les Jardins, Jan points towards the large burn pit, as well as a new collection of rental cars, which have appeared overnight. They are all loosely parked on the grassy area near the burn pit. He tells us they are for the the extra Gendarmes who will be arriving shortly. The other thing I notice right away is the growing collection of garbage bags littered along one of the two entrances into the neighborhood. The bags, while unsightly, have been purposely piled there as a security measure. They completely block one of the entrances.

There is only one way into and out of the neighborhood.

Alain takes a left onto the N7, and as we crest a steep hill, we have a panoramic view of the northeast corner of the island. The immediate impact of the widespread destruction silences all of us. There are massive shipping crates, battered and scattered all over the landscape. The land is stripped of vegetation and various sailboats lie in ruin after being blown thousands of yards from their moorings.

Our silence continues as we travel to the first main shopping center and the Mount Vernon district. Modern shops and businesses have been replaced by twisted metal beams, shattered window fronts and chaotic piles of debris. The once beautiful and massive "Leader Price" grocery store looks like it has been blown up from the inside. The spider web of mangled steel beams appears to be rising out from the destroyed interior of the store. None of the store shelves are standing and the ground is piled deep with the building's collapsed exterior walls.

The explosive violence of the hurricane winds is on sickening display. The damage just doesn't end. I keep hoping to see some area that was magically spared. So far on our route, that hope is well, hopeless.

As we enter the neighborhood of Hope Estate, we see more annihilation. This is a residential area and every single building, home or structure has been completely decimated. There are no roofs on any of the hundreds of homes and complexes. Nothing has been spared. There are large areas of murky, dark water full of debris, the ripped-up tropical rainforest flora, as well as several boats. Home after home is damaged beyond habitation.

"How did anyone survive who lived here?" someone in the truck asks. None of us answer.

We slowly drive on past the main road that leads to Grand Case. The scale of the horror continues all around us. The sheer obliteration of this beach city is overwhelming. Hotels and restaurants that used to line the coast have disappeared. There are mounds of sand and building remains everywhere.

There are people on the porches of their roofless homes, some sitting on plastic chairs, and a few people walk the streets in a trance. They simply stare at us as we slowly drive by. I attempt to take a few snapshots with my cell phone, but the totality of the destruction is too much. I don't feel like photographing all this misery. Shanie reaches for my hand. She clasps it in both of her hands and pulls me close to her. I look at her, so brave and understanding. The connectivity of holding hands steadies me.

As we continue to make our way to Marigot, I now begin to assemble a true realization of the island-wide ruination. My mind races full speed towards the actuality that it could be several weeks before Shanie and I can be evacuated. I have no idea how the French authorities will handle the immediate and desperate needs of the people who live here, let alone two Americans looking to return home.

I remain silent as Alain drives slowly through the streets of Concordia. Many are flooded and several times we need to wade through deep, stagnant water. Much like Marigot, the streets are narrow and Alain has to maneuver the truck around piles of debris, including broken roof segments and shredded building materials.

The narrow streets bring us up to the damaged homes, business and apartments. They feel right on top of us. My nerves are shot and there is a pit in my stomach. This feeling is compounded by the distant stares of the locals who watch us pass.

Alain is not fazed by these glances and confidently navigates us towards the school. We make a right turn and immediately pull over to what looks like a two-story home more than a school. We are astonished to see the school is completely intact. Even the white picket fence that borders the school has been untouched by Irma.

We exit the truck and follow Jan as he unlocks the glass front door to the school. As we enter, Jan points to an office on the right and a breakroom. He tells us there are power strips in both rooms and to immediately begin charging our phones. Since we are on the French side, the power strips are 220 amps and Shanie and I will need power converters to charge our phones. Thankfully, Martine has brought extras and we line up phones, our lanterns and the rechargeable mosquito rackets. These ingenious tennis-looking rackets are strung with thin medal threads that carry enough electricity to zap any small flying pest to neverland. They have been a godsend for us after the hurricane due to the explosion of the mosquito population from all the standing water.

Shanie needs to use the restroom and asks Jan if any are functioning. We haven't had the use of a working toilet since the hurricane. We've been doing our business outside, just beyond the lower bungalow where we dug several holes for use as toilets. Without power to operate the pumps to remove the waste, digging holes was the safest and healthiest option.

He grabs an igloo cooler full of water and some bleach and leads her upstairs to a student bathroom. The water and bleach will flush the toilet.

After Jan showed Shanie the restroom, he went across the street to another home that was also surprisingly undamaged. As Martine and I swap out more items to be charged, Jan returns and tells us that the home has internet service and he has arranged for Shanie and I to send emails.

I waste no time, grab my cell phone and make my way across the street. The house has a small side yard with a picnic table and chairs. It's like this tiny part of the neighborhood had a protective bubble over it during the hurricane. It's very bizarre.

There are a few people occupying the seats and picnic table, so I opt to sit on the curb. Alain hands me a piece of paper torn from a little notebook with the name of the WIFI and the password. The password looks like a blockchain address with almost 20 different letters, numbers and symbols. It takes me several moments with my shaky fingers to correctly enter the password and log on.

Martine, Shanie and Alain soon join me on the curb. Martine is also desperate to let her children know they are safe. She is especially eager to connect with her son, Arnaud, who lives in Miami. Irma is projected to hit Miami and wants to warn him to evacuate the city.

For the next ten minutes I frantically send emails as well as messages using Facebook messenger. The short messages inform that Shanie and I are okay, but desperate for help to get off the island. Several friends miraculously happen to be online and respond. One of them provides the address of the US Consulate, which is collecting names of Americans on the Island. I quickly give him my and Shanie's passport numbers to see if he can work stateside on our behalf.

I send an email to my little sister, Anne Marie, letting her know we are safe but the situation on the island is dire and that we have no idea how to evacuate. I plead to her to communicate with my father-in-law, to see if there would be any possibility of rescuing us via naval helicopter. He was in flight school with the late Senator John McCain and, like the Senator, also served in Vietnam. So I think maybe, just maybe, some strings can be pulled to make this happen. I add that we have had no contact with the outside world and, although safe, feel isolated on the French side of the island. Additionally, we have no official information about any organized evacuations.

Since we have email, I try my luck and place a call to my father-in-law. Unbelievably, the line connects. Rod answers and I quickly unload about our situation on the island. He relays that evacuations are happening on the Dutch side near the American University, and perhaps we could get to that side of the island. I tell him I see no way to make it there. The destruction is too much, supplies have to be limited, areas of the island appear cut off, and we don't know if it is safe to travel to that location. I hand the phone to Shanie who was listening to most of the conversation and she reconfirms to him we are okay. The situation is bad, but we are safe with Alain and Martine.

This ability to communicate with people back home is a double-edged sword. While I'm relieved that our family knows we are safe, it also magnifies the feeling of desperation and isolation. On the drive to the school from Villa Haiku, I witnessed massive widespread destruction on an island where I am not a citizen. I am a trapped, helpless foreigner.

After several more minutes, Alain and Jan urge us to leave, but I really don't want to let go of this invisible safety line I have with the U.S.

"We need to go," Alain insists as he grabs my shoulder. I quickly interpret his body language, shut down my phone and hasten back to the truck. In my focus on sending out messages, I hadn't noticed that several people had collected around the house and it was definitely time to get out of there. Safely back in the truck, we slowly make our way out of Concordia and without incident return to Villa Haiku. At the entrance to the property, I jump out to open the security gate and watch as Alain drives the truck down to the lower parking area. After I close and lock the gate, I walk down the steep driveway mentally sending wishful thoughts to the universe for the island's safety and, as inane as it sounds, to any American ship to come ashore and rescue us.

A NUMBER 1

I t's been five days since the hurricane and we've made good progress salvaging Alain and Martine's clothing, valued paintings, and most of the family photos and keepsakes. We've also attempted to shore up the damaged buildings with the limited supplies and tools. The next steps in rebuilding/demolishing Villa Haiku will require heavy machinery and skilled tradesmen.

We are at a crossroads and it feels like we have approached the limits of our capabilities. After a lunch of ramen noodles, which Alain and Martine had never heard of prior to our arrival, and playfully teased us about, no one is motivated to tackle any more projects. There is also a concern about the level of mold growing with all the saturated clothing, bedding, and other debris still strewn about the cottages.

Alain, Martine, Shanie and I linger on the porch and gaze out to Orient Bay and the Caribbean Sea. From our elevated vantage point, the water looks beautiful. The sun is out, the sky is blue and various aqua shades of the water's call to us like Greek Sirens.

We chat about how a dip in the ocean might revitalize each of us and give us some renewed vigor. Alain pleads to make the most of the afternoon and drive down to the sea. He also mentions that Jerad, who has frequently checked on us over the last several days, told us his pool is clean and we could spend part of the afternoon with him.

As we load into the truck, Shanie notices some smoke rising from an area close to the beaches.

"I wonder what's burning over there?" she asks the group.

"Probably burning debris piles. It's the only way to handle it all," Alain responds.

We agree because there currently is no alternative means of removing the colossal amounts of debris littered everywhere. All civil services have stopped since the hurricane and don't seem to be returning anytime soon.

Alain drives like we are in a hurry. He is swerving around piles of roofing, fractured trees and bags of garbage. It consistently surprises me how fast Alain drives his truck. You think he was helming a Porsche on a racetrack and not a 4x4 on roads that suffered a Category 5 Hurricane.

When we arrive at the security gate for the neighborhood, the piles of garbage have swelled to several feet in height and cover the entire entrance lane into neighborhood. The collection of garbage is staggering. The stench and buzzing flies are shocking.

We drive through the gate, cross the N7, and enter another security gate to the Orient Beach Neighborhood. The residents have also attempted to block much of this access lane. Several washing machines and piles of debris are placed at various opposing points along the roadway. This forces any vehicle to snake through the entrance at a very slow pace.

Alain parks close to the beach and, once where thriving shoreline businesses operated, there is nothing left. Every single one of them disappeared from the storm surge.

There is a smoky haze drifting towards us as we walk the beach and it appears to be intensifying. Shanie covers her mouth and wants to immediately return to the truck. As if it couldn't get any worse. It does.

A fireman rushes towards us shouting that a house is on fire and we need to leave immediately. We hurry past a group of people, perhaps a family, who ignore the warnings and sit on their partially cleared porch. It appears that they are taking a break. A break from what, we have no idea. They sit and drink bottled water and completely ignore the warning shouts.

We hurry past a mangled car awkwardly on its side. The tires are gone, the windows smashed and every inch of it has been beaten and battered.

More and more firemen arrive as we climb into the pickup truck. Alain slams the truck into reverse and guns it off the curb. The urgency of the danger is palpable, so we are tense and anxious to get back to Villa Haiku.

As we drive out of Orient Bay, the staggering damage and now house fire make me feel anger, frustration and even sadness. No one has escaped the devastation of Irma; it is affecting every single soul on the island. I've seen disaster movies and the directors do a great job of re-creating horrific damage from tornados, storm surge, natural and unnatural forces. But when you see it first hand, smell it and feel it, it is another level of apocalyptic dread.

A rhythmic clicking sound brings me out of my thoughts. The sound is emanating from somewhere outside the vehicle.

"Do you hear that clicking?" I question Alain.

He assures me that it is probably a rock wedged in one of the truck's thick "off road" tires.

"I've heard that before, shouldn't be a big deal."

We continue driving out of the neighborhood, snaking past the washers and dryers before stopping at the N7. Suddenly, a man starts pounding on Alain's driver's side window. Alain lowers the window and the man points to the drivers' side tire and shouts we have run over a large metal object. The object is sticking out of the tire and the tire is going flat.

"Fuck," Alain and I say in unison.

It is a silent and tense drive up the hill to Villa Haiku. This is the only working vehicle we have, and we have no idea if there is a spare.

At the security gate I exit the truck as Alain hands me the keys to unlock it. I slide the large gate back. As Alain turns to enter the property, something glints off the front tire. He continues down the driveway to the parking area by the bungalow. I close and lock the gate and proceed after them. It's about 2:00 p.m. and the heat of the day is oppressive. I'm drenched and my nerves are raw.

I walk up to the truck as Alain is getting out.

"Did you put on the parking brake?"

He assures me he has pulled up the hand brake. We scan the flat front tire for the metal object. It is nowhere to be found. So, I head back up the driveway to locate it. I slowly walk up the driveway to the security gate scanning for any large metal object. Luckily, at this point after the storm, we have cleared most of the storm debris from the pavement, so it should be easy to spot. I search all around the security gate to no avail.

About two-thirds of the way down the driveway, I spot the object. I reach down to pick it up and cannot believe what I find. It is a six-inch metal number "1" from a house address and probably mounted into brick or concrete near the front door. A three-inch steel post sticks out perpendicular from the backside.

The number probably had been lying on the ground with the

metal mounting post sticking straight up in the air when we ran over it, the long cylindrical mounting post piercing through the rubber tread and steel belts.

I pick it up and am surprised by the weight of it.

"No fucking way." Responds Alain as I hand him the object. "I thought these tires were impenetrable."

I again ask Alain if he put on the parking park as I walk around to the back of the truck to look for the jack. He assures me it is on.

Searching for the jack, we scan the bed of the truck, pushing away the shovel and garbage bags. I brush my hands over the wheel wells looking for an access door or something as Alain goes to the driver's side door, opens it and pops the hood. He searches the engine compartment. It's not there either.

"Do you have the owner's manual?" I shout.

"No, never got one from the previous owner."

"Fuck," I quietly exhale.

Alain and I then turn our attention to the passenger bench seat of the cab. He starts to try and pull the back of the bench seat down. Lifting up the headrests and pulling at anything that looks like it would be the release. I see a short grey webbing strip and pull at it. It releases the back rest, revealing a storage compartment that holds a neatly organized black canvas bag.

I untie the canvas bag and remove the Jack, as well as three long black pipes. One of these pipes has a thin, one-inch steel piece on it, making the pipe end look like a "T." The other two pipes appear to lock into this pipe, so you can place the jack deep under the truck. Since there is no manual, we scan under the now flat driver's side front tire looking for the correct place to mount the jack. I've changed many tires and point to an area I think we should place the jack. Alain is skeptical, because the top of the jack doesn't appear to have the same molded grooves as where I want it to go. But like much of our time together during this ordeal, Alain and I calmly discuss our opinions. Each listening intently to the other person's ideas and thoughts and together agreeing on a compromise before moving forward.

Alain quickly starts raising the jack.

"Whoa, slow down. We need to first find the spare."

I take a deep breath and we head to the back of the truck. Alain is quick to scurry under the bed of the truck. He reemerges and tells me he will go look for the tools to unlock the tire.

"Slow, slow down. There has to be a way to lower the spare with the jack and the tools in the kit."

"Really?" He says, shrugging his shoulders.

"Oui, Oui," I reply in my bad French accent.

I slide under the bed and peruse the muddy spare. First of all, I am grateful there is a spare, but it's not the same brand or style as the other tires. I scoot back out from underneath and stand by the back bumper. After some quick scanning, I recognize a one-inch oval opening on the bumper. I slide back underneath the truck and now see some sort of rotating mechanism near the spare.

Grabbing the "T" pipe as well as one of the long black pipes, I insert the black pipe into the "T" pipe as I walk back to the rear of the truck. The "T" nestles perfectly into the rotating mechanism near the spare and it turns out that a neatly coiled chain uncoils lowering the tire.

Alain is amazed by all of this. "Small victories," I say to him. He smiles.

As I gently slide the tire towards the back of the truck, Alain raises the chain back to its original position. It easily recoils and we lock the mounting plate and chain back under the truck. The tire definitely has air and easily rolls to the front of the truck.

The tires on the Ford truck are beefy and we have to extend the jack quite a bit to remove the damaged tire. I lift it off the lug bolts and Alain rolls it to the side. I try to position the spare on the lug bolts, but it will not align.

"Fuck, you've got to be kidding me."

Alain and I look at each other. As I wipe the sweat from my eyes, he suggests raising the jack to its maximum position. I thought I had done that, but after a few more turns, the jack extends several additional centimeters.

"Let's see if we can slide the tire better onto the bolts now," he suggests.

After a silent prayer, I raise the tire and rotate it a few more times until it matches the lug bolt pattern. The tire slides on.

Alain who is also sitting on the ground turns to me and smiles, "Small victories!"

Indeed, as the jack lowers, we hold our breath. The spare now supports the weight of the truck, and to our joy, it holds the air.

Alain and I are soaking wet as we walk with our arms around each other towards our home beneath the severely damaged Pavilion. The roof held aloft by the grace of Buddha's head. Shanie and Martine hand us each a bottle of water as we seek shade underneath the patio. I eagerly sit down in the cooling shade savoring the water. I look out to the truck and the Caribbean Sea. "Small Victories".

Later that afternoon, a good friend of Alain and Martine's, Gerard stops in to check on us and give us an update about the fire that broke out in Orient Bay. He relays it was arson. A couple of looters broke into a beach home and were squatting there. When the owner returned, he confronted the two youths and, feeling threatened, left to find help. When he came back, the home was on fire. The youths laughing at him as they fled.

Gerard lights up a cigarette and passes one to Alain. As they smoke, Shanie hands me another water and whispers to me.

"I'm proud of you today. Nice job."

Every day through this ordeal, she has found a moment to say something encouraging, to show me that no matter what we are dealing with, we are together and unbreakable. I enjoy a long swig of water and look into my wife's eyes. I am blessed.

As we sit on the porch that afternoon, little do we know the very next morning we will test the limits of that spare tire on our tense journey to the Princess Juliana International airport and the hope of evacuation.

EVACUATION

L ater that evening, after replacing the flat tire, we drive down to the neighborhood meeting spot. For some reason, we feel it is important to attend, and to show strength and solidarity with our neighbors.

There are about 40 people present and everyone is on edge. Jan shouts over the crowd to bring the meeting to order.

"Ecoutez, s"il vous plait! Ecoutez s'il vous plat."

Alain has told us these nightly gatherings are usually attended by two Gendarmes. They provide updated information, and reassure everyone they are doing everything they can. Admittedly they're stretched to the limit with the crime and disorder on the island. The pair this evening consists of a tall, muscular gentleman and his female partner. Both appear exhausted.

The female officer does most of the talking as her partner protectively stands by her side. Shanie and I listen as best we can, but only understand a few French words and try to infer sense out of those. Alain occasionally translates for me, but he too is paying close attention to the information.

The female Gendarme thanks the commitment and diligence by the residents who help protect the neighborhood, and then takes a voluntary step back in anticipation of her next comment. In a stern voice, she reminds everyone that shooting a looter is against the law, and could result in arrest and severe charges. As expected, her comments do not sit well with the group and cause angry shouts and pointed comments. After Alain translates this information to me, I think to myself, how is this even possible? That residents defending their property against criminals would be more punishable than the perpetrators themselves?

"Ecoutez, s'il vous plait! Ecoutez s'il vous plat," Jan shouts to hush the crowd.

Regrettably, the female officer informs everyone that they will again not be able to post any Gendarmes at the entrance. The crowd erupts again with shouts and frustrated comments. Several neighbors turn away in disgust and walk towards their homes.

This causes the meeting to quickly disintegrate. Many of the neighbors are exhausted from their late nights guarding the entrance, as well as the constant struggle to repair their homes and live moment-to-moment without electricity and running water.

It's fascinating as I look at the composition of people assembled here. These are "everyday" citizens, families with young children and senior citizens. The number of women and children surprises me. These are not well-trained military veterans or ex-police. They are ordinary folks standing up to armed, roaming gangs. It's the unity of the group that protects the entire neighborhood. It's impressive.

As people walk away, Shanie, approaches the male Gendarme.

"Americana."

He nods, understanding.

She asks him for any information regarding evacuations for Americans.

"Maybe, planes taking Americans. Princess Juliana Airport," he tells her in his limited English.

That is all he says before turning to his partner. They discuss something as they get into their car. They drive across the N7 into the neighborhood of Orient Beach and disappear among the mounds of wreckage.

This is the first we've heard of any evacuations and frankly, are stunned by its implications. I look to Martine and Alain and see the revelation is causing mixed emotions.

We walk back to Alain's truck. In the enveloping darkness of night, the headlights focus our eyes on the devastation alongside the road. The intertwined heaps of dead trees, tangled piles of vegetation and debris that once was civilized life. We are silent.

At the top of the hill, I get out to open the gate. Alain drives through and proceeds down the driveway. I close the gate. It slides easily and locks. I observe the growing flames from the bonfire as well as the placement of two cars with emergency lights at the community entrance. As the flames spark into the night, a sense of pride and belonging fills my heart. I am grateful to these fathers, mothers, brothers and sisters who tirelessly protect us.

I make my way to the porch to find Alain, Martine and Shanie. Alain is the first to break the silence. "In the morning, we'll drive you to the airport."

For the next hour, over pouring wine, cheese, laughs and tears we openly discuss all the feelings associated with Shanie and I evacuating. In the past week, we have shared every joyous, successful, "small victories" moment Hurricane Irma threw at us. These life-changing events are a powerful glue that permanently bond us together.

The only time we ever discussed actually leaving was a few days prior when we heard the Grand Case Airport had begun flights to Guadeloupe. These flights were just available to the seriously injured and women with small children, but if we could somehow get Shanie aboard a plane, she might be able to acquire any available supplies. There was never a mention of us both leaving.

Logically, it makes sense. There isn't more Shanie and I can physically do to repair the open roofs and blown-out windows on the property.

Additionally, it is no longer safe to enter the various buildings to remove any remaining wet and damaged clothes, papers and keepsakes. The heat, humidity and rain is rapidly accelerating the growth of mold.

We are also dealing with a finite supply of clean water and food. Martine and Alain had good pre-hurricane provisions, and Shanie and I brought a substantial amount of drinking water and food with us, but if Shanie and I evacuate, all these supplies should better aid in sustaining Alain and Martine.

There has been no steady government assistance with food and water. Worse yet, there is no indication the situation will improve in the near future.

We pour more wine and the conversation shifts to the security situation at Villa Haiku. Each night we stow away the porch table, the four chairs, propane tank and utility table, used water bottles, mops, shovels, buckets, anything that indicates people are living here and have life-sustaining supplies. The idea is if looters come onto the property, they will first be presented with the near complete demolishment of the buildings. If that doesn't deter them, they will not find any obvious signs of people living here. They will be confronted with locked and strong steel hurricane shutters, and hopefully decide to move on.

The lower bungalow, with a set of the doors blown off, remains unsecured. If looters decide to enter this building, they will only encounter piles of furniture and debris. If they want anything, their clamorous scavenging will be an early warning to us that there are people on the property. What we would do then is unknown. Luckily, we haven't had to confront a group of marauders.

We continue to enjoy the wine, and I watch as Alain seems to be drinking more than usual. He suddenly becomes boisterous and questions the need to store and secure any of the furniture and supplies each night.

"I don't see the reason," he challenges the table.

"What if they steal our propane tank? It's been vital to us having hot food and coffee?" I reply to Alain as I look to Shanie and Martine for support.

"They could also use the tank to smash into the apartment or throw it through your truck windows. I don't understand why you would want to risk any of that?"

But Alain is adamant there is no need to secure the property every night. He then recants about when he was a logistics coordinator for Air France and was relocated to Central Africa.

"I was kidnapped twice. I've had a machine gun pointed to my head," Alain tells us while using his fingers to mimic a gun pointing to his head.

"No fucking way? What?" I question him.

He describes how a friend of Martine's had to once hide under the stairs with her baby as an armed militia broke into their home and swept through their house.

Martine sets her drink down and begins to share a story of when Alain was kidnapped at gunpoint from a local county club. She describes how he persuaded her he would be safe on the golf course because the foursome included other Air France employees and the country club had armed security. Even though there was unrest in the area, Alain felt the guards at the Golf course would be all the protection necessary.

She tells us how he took his cell phone and assured her that everything would be fine. After several hours of not hearing from him, she became very nervous and made several calls to the local office of Air France. They had not heard from him either and too were concerned and began to make inquires. Several more hours passed, when finally, a call came in from Alain's cell phone number. But it wasn't him. It was the kidnappers.

They were demanding money and eventually placed Alain on the phone to speak with Martine. He again reassured her that he was in no "real" danger and thought he would be released soon. After a few more hours of captivity, the kidnappers released Alain and his associates. They all made it back to Alain's jeep and were able to return to the house.

By retelling these stories, Alain explains why he is not nervous at all about any marauders. He will rely on his ability to defuse any situation by talking with intruders as people. By being "human" to them, like he had done several times in Africa.

"I'm not sure I would solely depend on talking your way out of a situation," I reply, adding, "It's fine, if you want to try that, but why let someone just walk on the property and steal the propane tank. It doesn't make any sense to me. I think you're inviting trouble."

"Come on, Alain, it's not hard to wonder about the growing strife between those who have a roof, food, and water compared to those unfortunate citizens who do not. At what point will desperate people need to do desperate things."

He continues to plead his case about leaving everything out at night and says they'll be fine.

In frustration, I get up from the table and say my "good nights." We agree to be on the road by 6:00 a.m.

Shanie enters the bedroom a short time later and we begin to sort through our clothes and items. From Shanie's military up-bringing, she is pretty certain if we get evacuated on a C130, we will be allowed just one bag apiece, so we have to decide what to leave behind.

My wife and I work for about an hour organizing our clothes as well as sorting the various supplies we stored in the bathroom and bedroom closet. We line the extra water bottles against the bedroom wall, so Alain and Martine will have easy access to them.

Before the hurricane, we decided to hide water bottles through-out the apartment. This was a preventative measure in case part of the apartment became uninhabitable.

We also thought if marauders came in search of water, we would show them our supply in the kitchen and hope that would be enough.

I turn my attention to our snorkel gear and organize it on an empty shelf in the closet. As I place my snorkel gear bag on the shelf, I can't help but think about our first morning on the island which seems like a long, long time ago.

I place a wish to the universe. A wish that I can return to Saint Martin and snorkel the reef in Orient Bay with Alain.

Shanie and I don't say much as we clean our bedroom and place a pile of supplies we'll leave behind. This bedroom has been our sanctuary and our refuge before the hurricane, during and after. While we are happy at the thought of evacuation, we are torn about leaving our friends.

"They'll be okay, they're strong," Shanie confirms to me.

"As are you, my dear!" I reply crawling under the mosquito net to hug my brave wife.

***

The morning is quiet. I get out of bed and open the hurricane shutters without making too much clatter. The air is warm and the pre-dawn light is soft and welcoming.

I bring out Shanie's suitcase and my backpack, placing them next to Alain's truck. I'm ready to get on the road, but unfortunately, Alain is moving achingly slow this morning. At six o'clock, our projected time of departure, Alain finally wanders out of their bedroom. He is rubbing his forehead and is battling a hangover. His bloodshot eyes and pained movements clearly let us know we aren't leaving anytime soon. Alain ignites the propane stove to make coffee. Martine comes out from the kitchen with a baguette and some pasta. She asks me to arrange the table and chairs so we can sit down for a proper breakfast. There seems to be no hurry in departing and no one questions or discusses the urgency of leaving for the airport.

Alain brings over the hot coffee and the tension from last night's disagreements seems to abate in concert with the rising Caribbean sun. I look across the table and our ragged bunch, with unkempt hair, dirty fingernails, worn and sweat-stained clothes, and tired faces. I'm proud. It has been six rough days of fear, anxiety and primitive living. Yet, we are still a united team. A team thankful to have been together.

The sense of urgency finally sets in with the group and we quickly clean up the breakfast dishes and pile into the truck. Shanie and I in the back, Martine in the front with Alain driving.

As soon as we clear the gate to Villa Haiku, Alain guns the engine and begins to barrel down the road, swerving to miss dead tree stumps and garbage piles.

"Alain...you have to slow down," I plead to him. "Remember the spare tire!"

He slightly eases off the gas pedal. As we near the front entrance, a suspicious pickup truck passes us as it enters into the community.

"Who are those guys?" Martine asks.

"We need to follow them." Alain replies and does a quick U-turn to trail them.

Their truck is moving fast through the neighborhood, so Alain accelerates to keep up as he makes a sharp left turn onto a windy residential street. The road is clogged with piles of debris and pockmarked with several large potholes. Alain drives into one of the potholes with the spare front tire.

"Slow down! Slow down... Alain! You'll blow the front tire!"

Somehow the spare tire keeps its air. Alain also feels the intense impact of the pothole and slows down. He finally starts to drive more defensively, avoiding potholes and watching his speed. We drive up a short hill and spot the truck parked in a driveway. The four men are loading broken trees and branches into the bed of their vehicle.

"They're just landscapers." Martine replies, exasperated.

Alain agrees and turns the truck around to drive back towards the entrance of Les Jardins.

"We should let Jan know about the landscapers, let's stop by his house," Martine says to Alain. His house is by the community's entrance gate, so Alain pulls over to the curb as Martine jumps out and runs up to the door.

She disappears into his house and a few minutes later returns to the truck.

"Jan had also seen those guys drive in. He thought they were gardeners as well." Martine adds as Alain puts the truck into gear.

He drives out the entrance, turning left onto the N7. We don't go more than a few hundred yards when I notice a car parked alongside a tall retaining wall. A man and a woman exit the vehicle, go to the trunk, open it and remove several overstuffed black garbage bags. They abruptly toss them alongside the retaining wall before returning to their car. Without hesitation or the appearance of any guilt for dumping their garbage, they wave to Alain and Martine.

We proceed another quarter of mile when Martine frantically tells us we need to return to Villa Haiku.

"I forgot to take my heart pill."

"What?" "Seriously?" Alain replies in disbelief. They begin to converse in short terse sentences in French that Shanie and I can't understand. But from the intonations, it's obvious Alain is not happy with the idea of turning around.

"Alain, don't you understand the stress of all this, I need my pill," Martine pleads.

They go back and forth with each other in French for a bit until I can't take it anymore.

"Let's just go back and get her pill," I appeal to Alain.

Without a reply, Alain does a quick U-turn in the middle of the N7. He speeds back to Villa Haiku. Martine and I get out of the truck and we both run into the apartment. She locates her pill bottle and a bottle of water.

Within minutes we are again traveling along the N7 towards the Grand Case Airport. It's now closer to 7:30 a.m. and already there is a long line of cars on the access road for this French airport. Crowding the line of cars are hordes of people walking towards the makeshift terminal. They carry whatever they can in suitcases, duffle bags, brown grocery bags, shopping carts and baby strollers. The line consists of families with young children, elderly couples, as well as small groups of females.

"It looks like the military has finally arrived," Shanie points out as we see soldiers in green camo style uniforms armed with AK-47s lined along the single runway. Each soldier is stationed about every 100 yards and stoically looks at the masses of people shuffling past.

We continue along the N7 as it starts to make its way west before turning south to drop into Marigot. As we pass the turn-off to Anse De Marcel, the traffic comes to a complete halt. The roadway is jammed with cars moving in both directions. I grab the rooftop handrail and tensely squeeze it. My thoughts are in a gale force storm of anxiety. We left Villa Haiku later than expected, had to turn around, and now we are stuck in traffic. I wonder if we will miss any departing planes for America.

As we inch along the roadway, I notice the store that our taxi driver, Joyce, had first pulled into just eight days ago on our evacuation from Anse Des Sables to Villa Haiku. My tension breaks for a bit as I'm happy to see the same old man sitting on the concrete wall.

Just past the market is an open bread shop. The owners passing out loaves of bread to anyone who wants one. The people are orderly and not aggressive as the loaves are being handed out. We assume the owners are not charging anyone for the bread; A beautiful sign the people of the island are looking out for each other.

A little farther down the road a military officer directs Alain to pull over to the far-right side of the road. Within a few moments of getting to the side, I feel the earth start to shake as well as loud rumblings approaching us from somewhere just over a hill that rises before us. I roll down my window and stick my head out for a better view.

The first thing cresting the hill is a soldier appearing to float high above the roadway. He is wearing a dark blue military uniform with a red beret and a sub-machine gun strapped across his shoulder. As he seemingly floats towards the top of the hill, the large urban assault-style tank he is riding on comes into view. Several more assault tanks are in tow. As the lead tank passes us, the turret-riding soldier never strays his eyes from what's in front of him.

"Well fucking finally," Alain says to us as I close my window to lessen the noise and clatter from the tanks.

"Thank god. It's about time." Martine adds.

Once the procession of the tanks passes, we are allowed back onto the road and continue traveling the N7. We crest another hill where a group of 20-30 people are holding their phones extended high in the air in hopes to grab a signal. This is one of the higher points on the islands and the cell company, Orange, used to have a tower here.

The traffic begins to lessen as we drive into Marigot. The main road through the town center is still flooded and wherever there isn't standing water there are heaps of beach sand. Most of the palm trees have snapped in half or are horribly disfigured at odd angles. Debris piles litter the landscape along with several sail boats that have blown aground.

This is Shanie's and my first look at Marigot since the hurricane and it's eerily hard to recognize businesses or landmarks. The road ahead disappears into a pool of dirty sea water. Alain fearlessly drives through the flooded road. The water splashes up around us and I pray there isn't a large pothole or metal fragment submerged below the waters.

"Billy, look, over there you can make out the "Le Beach Hotel,"" Shanie says.

The damage to the hotel mirrors much of what we've already witnessed. The glass atrium atop the roof is completely blown out, only twisted metal frames remain. The roof is also severely compromised and the three dormers that lined the roof have been blown off. Many of the units are also missing their front doors. The parking lot is littered with broken palm trees, flipped over cars and piles of trash.

Alain makes a left turn and we pass the condo complex Shanie and I had looked at before Irma. Amazingly, the roof and structure look intact.

"Let's stop and take a picture," Shanie suggests.

"We need to keep going to the airport. Let's not stop," I interject, abruptly.

"Billy, you need to relax. We are almost to the airport," Alain shouts back to me.

"I just don't see the need to stop. We can always check the internet later for images of the building!" I reply peering over my shoulder to look at the complex, but to also hide my anger.

My outburst causes a silence to settle over all of us. The traffic is light, but there are lots of people walking the streets and hitch-hiking along the road. Alain pulls over to the side of the road.

"What's going on? I ask.

"Just giving this guy a lift," he responds as he signals for the hitchhiker to jump into the bed of the truck.

I shake my head in disbelief at Alain, but there is nothing I can do. I grasp the roof handle above my window tighter to control my frustration.

We continue to travel Rue de Holland and cross the border into the Dutch controlled part of the island. There are no guards, gates or checkpoints to stop and go through. Almost immediately after crossing the border we come to a roundabout that is blocked with randomly situated orange cones and carelessly placed yellow warning tape. The first exit off the roundabout is for the airport, but it is also barricaded with the yellow tape and pylons.

Alain stops the vehicle. The hitchhiker pounds the roof to let us know he is jumping off. He gets down, walks around the makeshift barrier and heads to a destination unknown to us.

"What should we do?" asks Martine.

To dramatically answer her, Alain shifts the pick up into drive and proceeds to jump the curb, swing around the cones and breaking through the yellow tape. He accelerates as he takes the first exit right on the roundabout, which leads to airport road and the elevated, half-mile long Simpson Bay Causeway Bridge.

"Are we sure this is safe? There is no one else on this bridge," cautions Martine.

Littered all along the bridge sit destroyed sailboats. It's like a sickening slalom course as we swerve around grounded, expensive sailboats. Several have masts that are either snapped in half or missing. There are gaping holes in many of the hulls along with mangled stays and blown-out port windows. In the bay, we can see that many of the sailboats have completely sunk. Their bare masts sticking out of the water like a tombstones marking their burial at sea. It's amazing and grotesque at the same time.

We remain quiet as Alain continues to drive around the damaged sailboats and I pray the bridge isn't severely compromised. A vision of the bridge giving way as we plummet into Simpson Bay to our deaths after suffering through so much already seems completely unfair to me, so I rapidly blink my eyes as a way to change the channel in my thinking.

As we near the end of the bridge, we see a massive, grounded, ocean-going vessel. The rust color hull towers above us, merely feet from the road. A few yards farther, we see what was probably a recently refurbished old wooden pirate ship. The beautifully painted ship is a complete loss as it is awkwardly pitched to one side against the rocks, flooded.

Alain enters another roundabout and takes the first exit to the right, which leads to the Princess Juliana Airport. The road parallels the main runway as a 737 taxis towards the terminal. The right side of the road borders Simpson Bay where several rental car companies and their rental fleets were. Many of the rental fleets are destroyed. They are either upside down with shattered windows, while others are buried under rubble and flotsam.

Just off the shore line are the remains of two large floating restaurants. One lies on its side swamped in the murky water. The other, a few yards deeper into the bay is completely submerged. As we near the parking lot for the airport we discuss alternate plans in case we do not get evacuated. Shanie and I are prepared to sleep at the airport tonight. And if after tomorrow, we still don't get onto a plane, we will make our way back to Villa Haiku. We insist they drop us off and return immediately to Villa Haiku.

Alain drives into the main entrance and we now see the crowds and crowds of people standing in various lines, many holding red and white colored umbrellas to shade them from the hot sun.

As Alain pulls into the main parking lot, he stops to wait for a vehicle in front of us to unload the passengers. Shanie notices a soldier walking towards the terminal and decides to abruptly exit the truck.

"I'm going to find out what's going on."

I suddenly feel panicked. I'm with Alain and Martine, and my wife is quickly disappearing into a sea of soldiers and evacuees.

"I'm going to follow her," I yell, grabbing my backpack and a bottled water.

"Thank you both so much for everything," I hollar back before slamming the back door. I sprint in the direction Shanie was running and quickly locate her. She is chatting with a young soldier wearing khakis and a blue DLF armband. DLF stands for the Dutch Liberation Force, and with their presence, we feel like things are getting somewhat under control.

She is peppering him with questions, so I take a moment to take in the situation at the airport. It is a busy, crowded scene. There are a number of clean-cut, young soldiers with holstered firearms, families with young children, groups of teenagers, young couples, as well as a surprising number of retirees. Several travelers are loaded with many suitcases while others only have a backpack and small purse. The general sense is the operation has been in effect for a couple of days. It's relatively organized and calm.

There are two large cement block walls protecting the single entrance to the back of the main terminal. The cement walls are separated by a tall, chain-link fence that has a matching chain-link access door. There is a lot of activity near the terminal as soldiers come and go carrying supplies of bottled water, airport personnel move about and several fork lifts drive back and forth transporting cargo from areas I can't see behind the cement block walls. The brand-new terminal's outward structure looks okay, but no one is going in or out of the terminal. I surmise the roof is gone and completely flooded.

On the left side of the block wall are strips of duct tape spelling out "Dutch." Next, to that, also about six feet in length, is the word "France." On the right side of the brick wall, also in duct tape is "USA." These haphazardly written country denotations separate the crowds into different holding areas.

"Please, get in the line for Americans," the soldier politely directs Shanie and I.

"Do you know if they're evacuating us?" She asks.

"Sorry, no details, just go stand in line over there with the other Americans. Good luck. "

"Thank you for being here." Shanie replies as he turns to meet up with another soldier.

"Okay, let's go stand in line...where are Martine and Alain?"

"I don't know, after you took off, I just jumped out of the truck to follow you," I reply.

We cross over several parking stalls and step over a curb to get onto a wide sidewalk that has been divided into two separate lanes via ropes and stanchions. There are about 20 people in one of the lanes. The other line contains at least a hundred or so travelers.

We walk up to the less crowded line. "Do you know which line is for Americans?" I ask a short, heavy-set man with rather pale skin.

"You're in it," he says.

"Cool...there aren't many of us?" I inquire.

"Yeah, a lot of Americans were evacuated yesterday. I had a friend text me he got off the island on a C130. He was flown to Puerto Rico."

"Do you know anything about any flights today?" I ask.

"No, nobody seems to know anything. I heard all the USA planes had been diverted to Miami to help with the evacuations there ahead of Irma's arrival," he responds pulling out his cellphone.

"Fuck dude, your phone works? Would you let me make a call? Please, man, we need to contact my wife's parents."

"Yeah, give it a try...it probably won't work...I've been trying since I got up today."

He hands me his phone and I punch the numbers for Shanie's mom. I put the iPhone to my ears and wait. And wait. And wait. Nothing happens. I hang up and try again, still nothing.

"Ah, fuck, bummer." I hand the phone to the gentleman. "Nothing...thanks anyway, maybe you'll let me try later?"

"Yeah, no problem."

The sound of a KLM airplane landing draws everyone's attention and, as it taxis back towards the terminal, we see a line of people moving towards the gate from the "Dutch" side of the parking lot.

As we watch the line of people shuffle towards the gate, I hear Alain call out from behind me, "Here you are."

"We just had to check on you two to see if you needed any help," Alain smiles.

"I think we're good. And it looks like we should get evacuated today," I confidently answer.

Martine hands Shanie an umbrella. "Here, take this, I see everyone else has umbrellas, you can use this one."

For the next several minutes, we hug each other and snap a selfie they promise to post on their Facebook page as soon as cell service returns. Alain and Martine try and persuade us they should stay until they see us actually board a plane, but we insist they get back on the road.

"What if you don't get on a plane?" Asks Alain.

"We'll be okay. There are lots of soldiers here and other Americans. We'll figure it out," I reassure him.

We hug each other one more time and watch as they make their way across the parking lot to the familiar burnt orange pick-up truck.

Shanie and I look to each other with tears in our eyes. It is difficult watching them drive off, but we know it is the right, albeit painful, decision to evacuate.

An Air France plane lands and almost immediately, similar to the KLM plane, a line of people begin to make their way towards the entrance gate. This line of French citizens is to our immediate left and we watch as another group of evacuees prepare to board a plane and fly off the island. All of us are eager to get home. Watching others fly away is not easy.

We wait patiently in the blistering heat with little or no word about any military or commercial flights arriving to take us to the USA, via Miami or Puerto Rico.

In fact, our line has not moved for several hours and has steadily become more crowded. As streams of people arrive in line, they begin to press up to the people standing in line ahead of them. Tempers begin to flare as hot, tired, desperate and aggravated people are being jammed closer together. The situation is rapidly escalating, so Shanie jumps out of the line and runs up to the soldier she had previously spoken to. He listens as she dramatically points to the American line and then forcibly leads him to us.

"You all need to be patient! No pushing! Everyone, please take a step back!" He orders. His commands have the desired effect and immediately everyone takes a few steps back, which opens up everyone's personal space enough to stem the tempers.

"Can I help you with that suitcase?" I ask a frazzled, but stylish lady as she tries to take a step back while holding an umbrella, trying to control a roller bag as well as large, partially unzipped canvas duffle bag.

"Cheers," she replies in her pleasant British accent as she hands over her umbrella and roller bag.

Her husband, who is returning from getting a few water bottles from a Dutch soldier, approaches Shanie and I.

"I'm Ed and this is my wife Judith," he says handing a water bottle to Judith and one to my wife.

"Thanks for the water. I'm Shanie and this is Billy."

"No one knows anything about any planes for Americans. It looks like we might be here for a while," he states.

Ed and Judith are from London and own a home on the island. Ed then begins to describe their ordeal during and after the storm.

"Every window in our home shattered. There was glass everywhere," Ed recounts in startling detail how their million-dollar home had hurricane-proof windows, Kevlar shades as well as steel hurricane shutters, but none of it mattered. The force of the winds and flying debris smashed every window on their second floor sending them fleeing to a small wine cellar for safety and survival.

"The amount of shattered glass was incredible. It was like three or four inches thick in some places on our floors." Ed shakes his head in disbelief and continues describing how their massive slate kitchen table weighing hundreds of pounds had flown across the entire length of the kitchen before slamming into a far wall.

Even with the extent of damage, their plan was to stay in their home and coordinate the rebuilding. They had stocked up with plenty of food and water and had an industrial strength generator on the property. It was the size of a minivan, full of diesel fuel and could power their home for at least 30 days. Up until a day ago, they were cleaning up the glass and making headway until the generator died. Ed tried everything he could, but couldn't get the generator restarted.

"There was no way we could live in our home without running water and power," adds Judith.

She describes how they boarded up windows and secured the house the best they could before making their way to a local hotel. At the hotel, they were told horror story after horror story of violent incidents involving tourists and locals. At another hotel on the island, a group of men were masquerading as a security force. These men would knock on a guest's doors, explain who they were and once the occupant opened the door, the men would rush into the room, pistol whip them and rob them of jewelry, watches, cash and clothing. These stories terrified Ed and Judith so they decided they were done with Saint Martin. Once they got off the island they were not coming back. Their property was up for sale. They didn't care if they would take a loss on it, they just wanted to be rid of it as well as be rid of Saint Martin.

As Judith retells her distressing story, the tropical sun is also taking a toll on her. She is unsteady and her color is draining. I suggest sitting on her rolling suitcase while I'll hold the umbrella directly over her.

Ed forces his wife to drink more water. His next move is to kneel down and pour the remainder into a small dish next to their zippered duffle bag. As if by magic, a small dog hiding in the tossed clothes suddenly pops his head out, sees the water and quickly starts to lap it up.

Judith explains that one of her friends had left a week prior to the hurricane and asked if they would care for "Ollie" until they returned.

But Judith and Ed are now leaving the island and felt obligated to take the dog with them to the owners' other home in Miami. Ollie is adorable and very friendly, so naturally he becomes an instant attraction with everyone around us. Quickly, introductions are made amongst several folks in our vicinity.

Our immediate group includes a salvage diver from Kentucky, a heavily tattooed, ex-Israeli special ops soldier, a charter boat sail captain and young college woman with red hair. Like Ed and Judith, each eager to share their tale of survival during the hurricane and the days that followed until they managed to get to the airport. The retelling of their ordeals feels like a cathartic way for all of us to bond while we wait in line.

"I have to go pee," Shanie looks at me. I'm a little stuck holding the umbrella for Judith, so I raise my eyebrows to let her know I can't go with her.

"I'll take her over by that tree," offers the sailboat captain.

My wife hands him the golf umbrella from Martine and together they walk over to a lone, but very large tree near the wall with USA written across it. My wife wastes no time as the captain provides some privacy using the umbrella to shield her. There are no porta-pottys to be found, and after six days without running water and electricity, basic human necessities become more important than decorum.

As they walk back, Shanie takes a detour to the front of the line. She recognizes the soldier from when we first arrived and is hoping for an update.

About five people in front of Judith and I stands a group of teenagers. They all seem to know each other and are crowding around what appears to be two men and a woman. One of the men has an official-looking binder and is using the hard surface to stamp paper. He shakes hands with the man and woman, then makes his way farther down the line.

"Does anybody need a notary? Anybody traveling with somebody else's kids?" He shouts to us.

For whatever reason, some parents can't leave the island yet, but want their friends to assist in evacuating their children. The notary seems completely aware of this and is making his way through the crowds. Several people with groups of children make their way to him and present their passports and paperwork.

Judith and I are distracted watching the notary as Shanie rushes back from the front of the line.

"We are leaving right now! There is a plane leaving for Panama City. We can get on it, but we have to go right now! Hurry!"

"What? How?" I ask.

"I'll fill you in later, but we need to go...NOW!"

Shanie provides a quick recap to our group about a plane taking Americans to Panama City. Much to our surprise, only Ed, Judith and the college co-ed want to give up their spot in line. The others will wait it out in the hopes the rumored US Military's C130 will soon arrive to fly them to Puerto Rico.

I grab our backpack and take Shanie's hand. My heart is pumping as we race up to the front and are allowed underneath the rope.

"It's Copa Airlines. They just announced they will fly any Americans to Panama City. We just need to find accommodations and a flight to the US from there," Shanie tells me as we hurriedly walk to the entrance gate we'd already watched so many other evacuees pass through.

We enter, and to our left, resting about 150 yards away on the tarmac, is a Copa Airline 737 jet. I don't remember this plane landing and am a bit flabbergasted to see it so close to the main terminal. It looks huge and beautiful. Two soldiers point us to a 4x8 cafeteria table that has been hastily set up to function as the Copa Airlines counter and immigration check. There are two airline workers looking at passports and handwriting the numbers on a paper log. The lady tells us we aren't allowed any bags or carry-ons aboard the plane.

"You can only take a few personal items, like medicines onto the plane," she tells us. The lady is calm and pleasant considering the desperate passengers she is dealing with.

Shanie quickly organizes what she needs and places everything in a green fanny pack. Then another worker takes our backpack and puts it into a large, clear plastic bag. He wire ties a baggage ticket to the top, rips off the bottom portion and hands me the perforated baggage ticket.

"This will be in baggage claim in Panama City," he tells us as he hurls my backpack onto the luggage cart.

"That was surprisingly simple," I say to Shanie as we continue to walk towards the jet.

As we make our way to the parked 737, Ed comes up from behind, clearly out of breath. "We had to leave Ollie behind. They wouldn't allow him on the plane. So, I had to run back to the line and persuade the young sailboat captain to try and take him if they are evacuated to Puerto Rico. Ollie has American papers, so it should be okay."

"There was nothing else we could do, we're hoping for the best," Judith chimes as she hurries to catch up to us.

For countless hours we have been standing on a sidewalk, exposed to the sun. Just 50 yards ahead of us, parked like it is also eager to get off this island, is the Copa Airlines jet, our escape from hurricane ravaged Saint Martin.

As a group, we stroll towards the stairwell to the plane. The Copa staff quickly separate males from females. Judith, Shanie and the co-ed go to the left as Ed and I are directed to the right. Ed and I are lightly frisked and then cleared to board. At the top of the stairs, I look back for my wife and the others as they are just approaching the female Copa attendant to have their purses checked.

Passing through the door into the plane, I'm totally surprised and almost lose my footing because of the impact of the cold blowing air from the planes air conditioning system. After 6 days of sweltering heat, humidity and primitive living, the cool air is staggering in its beautiful sensation on my sunburned skin.

Due to the natural delay in checking women's purses and personal items, the line for men moves much faster, and so, the aisle in the plane is not crowded. I easily make my way past rows of available seats. I quickly take advantage of an open exit row. Ed follows me and grabs the row of seats on the other side of the aisle.

I'm still in awe of the relief of cool air when I see Shanie enter the plane. Her reaction is also in awe of the amazing relief of the blasting cool air. She makes her way down the aisle. I rise out of my seat as she slides in next to me. Instantly, we grab each other's hand and take a moment to let our emotions catch up with us.
"I love you," she says.

"Love you, too," I reply.

Each person entering the plane experiences the same relief of the AC, and once they find their seats, become overwhelmed with the realization they are actually being evacuated. This reality, along with the range of emotions associated with being on this island during the storm and all the aftermath, causes several passengers to break down. The sad, desperate, and grateful tears spread throughout the plane. A loud wailing is heard from somewhere behind us that causes Shanie to squeeze my hand harder. We understand and sympathize for the myriad of reasons for those cries.

Our emotional and physical ordeal feels like it is almost over, I remove my ball cap and hide my face for a moment to collect myself. I then grab my cell phone to snap a selfie of Shanie and I. They say a picture can say a thousand words, and this photo is proof. The image captures Shanie and I leaning our heads towards one another, our eyes are closed, I have a shaggy beard and Shanie is clutching a water bottle. But what is really telling in the photo is the expression of sheer relief, sheer exhaustion and sheer love of each other.

"As soon as we get to Panama and a cell signal, I'll upload it to Facebook to let everyone know we have been evacuated," I say to Shanie. She blinks several times and for the first time during our entire ordeal has tears welling in her eyes.

More people continue to board, and we see that the last few have suffered various injuries during or after the hurricane. A few have gauze bandages wrapped around their heads, one has an arm in a sling and yet another tries to get down the aisle by clutching the tops of seats to steady herself. Her other hand clutching a pair of crutches.

Ed and Judith are settling into their seats. He has his tray out with a water bottle resting atop of it when all of the sudden, the lady in the seat directly in front of him releases her seat and violently tilts it all the way back into Ed's lap. This causes his water bottle to hit the floor and Ed explodes in anger.

"What are you doing?" He can't believe what she has done and is loudly berating her. Her husband rushes up from a few seats back and a Copa Airline worker also quickly makes his way down the aisle.

"I've been through a hurricane, my house is destroyed and the first thing you do is throw your seat all the way back! What is wrong with you?!!"

Her husband tries to defend her, but Ed wants none of it and gets up off his seat to go eye-to-eye with him. The Copa Airline attendant steps in between them and politely offers to move her to another seat. She obliges, but not before her husband gives Ed some choice words about his attitude.

This sudden outburst from Ed completely takes Shanie and I by surprise. Since meeting Judith and Ed, he has been a true gentleman, helpful, caring and calm. We credit it to the toll on having to abandon their home, leaving their friend's dog, and the sheer exhaustion of standing out in the sun for hours. The trauma of Irma has impacted all of us, in all sorts of charted and uncharted, emotional ways.

Fortunately, as quickly as the tempers flared, they settle when the airline attendant's pre-flight message comes over the PA. She lets us know that as soon as they close the doors and crosscheck them, we will taxi to the runway and immediately depart.

This causes everyone in the plane to start clapping. The applause continues as we make our way out to the single runway. The plane pauses for only a brief moment and then the pilot throttles the engines to full power for take-off. As the wheels lift off the runway, and 150 desperate evacuees lift off the island of Saint Martin, a cacophony of cheers, whistles, claps reverberate throughout the entire plane. This harmonious combination of full-powered jet engines, and shouts of joy from each and every passenger is perhaps the greatest melody I've ever heard and felt.

I look to my beautiful wife, whose strength and courage

through breast cancer and now through Hurricane Irma led us to this very moment. I am in awe of her.

We are safe and heading home.

I wish to thank Alain and Martine Pages. They allowed Shanie and I to stay with them during the worst hurricane to occur on the planet. They barely knew Shanie and had never met me, yet they opened their home and hearts to us. We became family. It's not too difficult to believe they probably saved our lives.

Shanie and I are forever grateful to you both.

EPILOGUE

I want to first thank all the readers for their wonderful comments about our story. The "shared experience" many of you expressed when reading about the sights, sounds, emotions and struggles of surviving Hurricane Irma, or any catastrophic event, as well as the difficulties after the storm touched me as much as my words touched you. Your outreach via social media or emails have made this journey so rewarding. Thank you.

Additionally, many of you posed thoughtful questions concerning Alain and Martine, the island of Saint Martin, Ollie, and what happened after Shanie and I returned to the United States. These and other questions only enrich this story and I hope to answer many of them now.

To begin, our Copa Airlines Evacuation flight flew us from Saint Martin to Panama City, Panama, not directly to the United States. In Panama, we would have to endure another four days of waiting until finally getting a flight to LAX. Because of Hurricane Harvey and Irma, the US ports of entry at the George Bush Intercontinental Airport in Houston and the Miami International Airport were closed. Ed and Judith, who were on the Copa Airlines flight joined us and also booked rooms at the Waldorf Astoria Hotel in Panama City. At $120 a night, it seemed like a bargain to stay at such a nice hotel.

While the hot shower, good food and shared company were

marked improvements from our survival days on Saint Martin, all of us just wanted to get home. Unfortunately for Ed and Judith, their scheduled flight to the U.S. was delayed another two days due to, of all things, a power outage at the Tocuman International Airport in Panama City. Sheesh, talk about testing one's moxie!

And what happened to Ollie? After quite the journey of his own, he was finally reunited with his owners. But I'm getting ahead of the story here.

Ed and Judith were forced to leave Ollie with one of the gentlemen in the evacuation line. Unfortunately, his US C130 military flight to Puerto Rico wouldn't allow pets on the flight. Remember at this point for many of the evacuees at the airport, they had been standing in line for over 12 hours, some much longer. He was forced to leave the dog, and decided the best chance for Ollie was to safely tether him to a nearby fence. The gentleman had also written a note providing the dog's name as well as the owners'.

But Ollie is a very charming and moderately lucky pooch. A local islander found Ollie, took him home and cared for him until his owners could get back on the island. Ollie was a bit of international sensation at this point, because while in Panama City, we read a newspaper from Miami that had printed the story about Ollie's plight. Ollie is now the legendary dog of Hurricane Irma.

More good news comes from Villa Haiku and the Pages. Alain and Martine have beautifully rebuilt their magical villa. Out of all utter devastation, there now rise stronger and considerably better-designed structures. They were able to rethink some of the building layouts and actually made significant modifications to increase the occupancy options. The rebuilding process took almost two years and constant vigilance on their part in overseeing the construction.

If visiting Saint Martin, please consider staying at Villa Haiku. Alain and Martine are incredible hosts and provide everything you would ever need for a sensational vacation. Yes, the Buddha statue is standing proud in the pavilion!

Shanie and I have been back to the island several times and are so impressed with the island wide reconstruction. The loving soul of the place remains firmly entrenched in the beautiful sand beaches, azure water and friendly smiles of all who you encounter.

Cheers!
Billy

ISLAND OF SAINT MARTIN

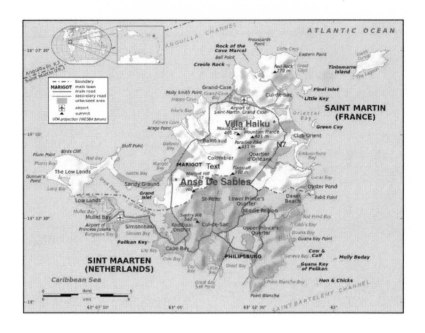

L-R, BILLY, SHANIE, ALAIN AND MAR-
TINE. 24 HOURS BEFORE IRMA

HURRICANE IRMA

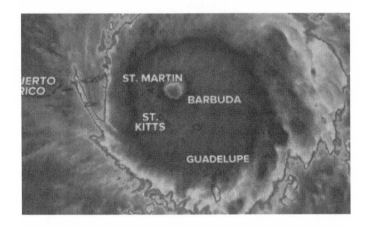

BUDDHA PREVENTING PAVILION ROOF
FROM TOTAL COLLAPSE

VILLA HAIKU PAVILION, KITCHEN
COTTAGE & CARPORT

SELFIE OF SHANIE AND I ON OUR COPA
AIRLINES EVACUATION FLIGHT.

BILLY NAHN AND SHANIE BANKSON RESIDE IN FOUNTAIN HILLS, ARIZONA.

65554931R00097

Made in the USA
Middletown, DE
08 September 2019